DINING SECRETS™

of

Indiana

Welcome...

to the sixth edition of "DINING SECRETS™ *of* Indiana."

The sixth edition will continue to delight you with an even greater number and variety of "dining secrets" throughout Indiana and its borders. Whether you're in the mood to try something different or just looking for some good old hometown cooking, you'll enjoy many of the newest additions in more wonderful locations and unique settings. For your added enjoyment, we have included some interesting things to do and see while traveling throughout the state if you have some extra time. For golf enthusiasts, we have provided a list of what we feel are some of the best golf courses in Indiana. You'll find these "extras" in the back of the guide.

The entire content of "DINING SECRETS™ *of* Indiana" was personally chosen by Poole Publishing and none of the restaurants or attractions were charged a fee to be included in the publication.

Through our own personal research and restaurant owner input, we have made every effort to insure that the information about each restaurant is correct. However, please be aware that changes do occur.

Poole Publishing
(317) 849-9199
(800) 401-4599

Location Map

The numbers next to each restaurant on the following pages correspond with the numbers on the map below.

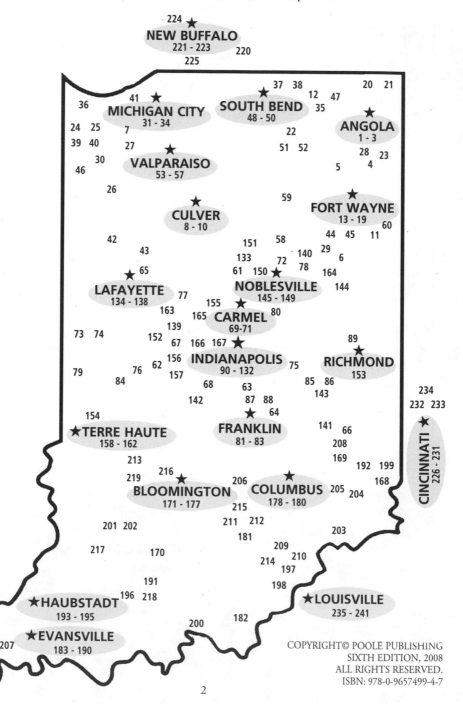

224
NEW BUFFALO
221 - 223   220
225

37 38   20 21
41   12 47
36   **MICHIGAN CITY**   **SOUTH BEND**   35
31 - 34   48 - 50   **ANGOLA**
24 25   7   **1 - 3**
39 40   27   22
30   51 52   28 23
46   **VALPARAISO**   5   4
53 - 57
26   59
CULVER   **FORT WAYNE**
8 - 10   13 - 19   60
42   44 45 11
43   151 58   29   6
133   140
61 150   72   78   164
65   **NOBLESVILLE**   144
LAFAYETTE   77   145 - 149
134 - 138   155
163   165   **CARMEL**   80
139   69 - 71
73 74   152   67 166 167   89
156   **RICHMOND**
79   76 62   **INDIANAPOLIS** 75   153
84   157   90 - 132
68   63   85 86
142   87 88   143
154   64
TERRE HAUTE   **FRANKLIN**   141 66
158 - 162   81 - 83   208
213   169
219 216   192 199
BLOOMINGTON   **COLUMBUS** 205 204   168
171 - 177   178 - 180
215
211 212
201 202   181
217   170   209
214   210
197
191   198
196 218
HAUBSTADT   **LOUISVILLE**
193 - 195   235 - 241
EVANSVILLE
207   183 - 190   200   182

234
232 233
CINCINNATI
226 - 231

Easy to Use!

The book is arranged so you will find it convenient to use as you travel around the state.

Locator Map
To identify the general location of a particular restaurant, look at the map on the left. The numbers on the locator map correspond with the numbers next to the restaurants.

Alphabetical Listing By Area
The front index is divided into four sections--Northern, Central and Southern Indiana, plus Border States The cities and towns are listed alphabetically under each section. When traveling through a particular area, you can check to see what restaurant is close by.

Restaurant Information
To assist you in planning your visit, each restaurant lists an address, phone number, meals served and days open and closed. CALL AHEAD FOR SPECIFIC MEAL TIMES.

Attractions
The attractions and golf courses are listed alphabetically by city as an easy reference when you are visiting a particular area.

Restaurant Index
If you know which restaurant you want to visit, refer to the alphabetical listing of restaurants and corresponding page numbers on the back pages.

Northern Indiana

Central Indiana

Southern Indiana

BORDER STATES

Michigan

Ohio

Kentucky

Northern Indiana

1. CAPTAIN'S CABIN SUPPER CLUB

3070 West Shadyside Road
Angola, IN 46703
(260) 665-5663
Open Tuesday-Sunday for dinner.
Credit cards accepted.

Built in the late 1800's, there is quite a history surrounding this old log cabin that is now a fine dining establishment. Originally a trading post, boarding house, ice house and fish house, it served as a convenient stop for early settlers and travelers. Today, you can relax and enjoy a superb lobster, seafood or choice steak dinner as you reflect on those earlier times in history.

2. CARUSO'S

2435 North 200 West
Angola, IN 46703
(260) 833-2617
Open Tuesday-Friday for lunch & dinner; Saturday for dinner;
Sundays seasonal. Closed Monday.
Credit cards accepted.

Family pictures adorning the walls leave no doubt that Caruso's is, in fact, family owned and family friendly. Caruso's has been serving "house made" classic Italian cuisine for over 30 years and is looked upon as an institution in the Northeast Indiana lakes region. Whether you choose pizza, pasta or Classico Italiano chicken or veal, you can be assured that only imported pastas and extra virgin olive oil from Italy are used to prepare the authentic Italian dishes. A unique menu item is Caruso's famous "Torpedoughs" that come with a choice of six different stuffings. There is also a nice variety of sandwiches, subs, salads, seafood and "steaks and such" listed on the menu.

3. LELLI'S HATCHERY

118 South Elizabeth Street
Angola, IN 46703
(260) 665-9957
Open Monday-Saturday for dinner. Closed Sunday.
Credit cards accepted.

The name of this restaurant originated from the fact that the building was actually a chicken hatchery in the early 1900's. Now you can enjoy fine dining in an intimate, formal setting, accented with midnight blue and pink colors, dim lighting, flowers, candles, and a baby grand piano. The Hatchery specializes in a fresh seafood menu plus steak, lamb and daily chef specials. Your favorite wine can be ordered from an extensive wine list, recognized with <u>Wine Spectator</u>'s Award of Excellence since 1991.

4. BREAD BASKET

115 North Main
Auburn, IN 46706
(260) 925-4257
Open Monday-Saturday for continental breakfast
& lunch. Closed Sunday.
Credit cards accepted.

This restaurant is located on the second floor of an old building just off the square in downtown Auburn. The light and airy interior has the atmosphere of a charming tea-room and bakery, accented with wooden floors, old signs and quilts on the walls. As you step inside, there are glass cases filled with several different kinds of cookies, homemade breads, and other dessert and coffee treats. The menu offers a wonderful variety of soups, salads, quiche, sandwiches on a choice of bread, pita or croissant, and seven different wraps--flour tortillas with different fillings.

5. ST. JAMES RESTAURANT

204 East Albion Street
Avilla, IN 46710
(260) 897-2114
Open Monday-Saturday for breakfast, lunch & dinner. Closed Sunday.
Credit cards accepted.

The Indiana Restaurant Association recognized the St. James as the oldest restaurant in Northern Indiana, named after the James family (no one knows where the "St." came from!) who built the original hotel in 1878. The Freeman family refurbished the old deteriorated hotel in 1948 and has continued to remodel and add rooms, making it the successful dining establishment it is today. The history of the building is documented in photographs displayed throughout the interior. St. James' broasted chicken tops the menu, but there are steaks, seafood, pork dinners and sandwiches as well. There are also some sinful desserts like Snickers pie, totally turtle pie, and chocolate suicide cake. A full bar is available with your favorite beverages.

6. BILLY ANN'S

113 North Main Street
Bluffton, IN 46714
(260) 824-8060
Open Tuesday-Sunday for dinner. Closed Monday. (Closed Sunday in summer.)
Credit cards accepted.

The entry to this Bluffton pub is decorated with stained glass windows depicting scenes of Native Americans riding horses and canoeing. More stained glass surrounds the lighting inside. The overall appearance is of a rustic barn, and church pews are used for seating in the booths. For those craving Mexican food, there is a variety of Southwestern and Tex-Mex items available. In addition, the menu offers a nice selection of salads, sandwiches, broiled haddock and steaks: filet, New York strip and teriyaki ribeye. Since this is a bar, you must be 21 to enter.

7. LUCREZIA

428 South Calumet Road
Chesterton, IN 46304
(219) 926-5829
Open daily for lunch & dinner.
Credit cards accepted.

Was the famous Lucrezia Borgia, subject of Donizetti's 1833 opera, a patron of the arts or a depraved woman? Is her reputation for wantonness and crime legend more than fact? What we do know is that Lucrezia, a product of Renaissance Italy, would appreciate and enjoy the food at this restaurant bearing her name! Picture driving through the countryside of Italy and coming upon an old one story, green wooden house on a corner. The windows are oval shaped, the floors are wood, the table tops are marble, and the rooms are small and intimate. Lucrezia, painted by a local artist, greets you as you enter and overlooks the bar where martinis are the specialty. Blackboards on the wall announce the daily specials: fish, pasta, chicken, salads and vegetables. Bread is brought to your table and can be embellished with roasted red pepper pesto. Pastas are available in many combinations, and the fish, lamb, salmon and veal entrees are truly special. For dessert, you may want to try the stuffed strawberries or the seasonal homemade tiramisu.

8. CITY TAVERN

415 East Lakeshore Drive
Culver, IN 46511
(574) 842-3300
Open Saturday & Sunday for breakfast; Friday-Sunday for lunch;
Tuesday-Saturday for dinner. Closed Monday.
Credit cards accepted.

The City Tavern offers the tastes of the city while at the lake. To start with, it boasts having the only sushi bar in the area! In addition to the typical breakfast offerings, the menu offers salmon and eggs, eggs and crispy crabcakes, turtle pancakes, and bruleed banana French toast. The "lite" entrees include chipotle-crusted grouper and steak with asparagus. There are bistro favorites like "Rarebit du Cite Tavern," comfort foods such as fettucine with meatballs, plus steak, fish and ribs. The restaurant has an aura of the city with art rather than posters decorating the walls and a smoke-free premium bar.

9. PAPA'S

824 North Lakeshore Drive
Culver, IN 46511
(574) 842-3331
Open Friday-Sunday for lunch; daily for dinner.
Credit cards accepted.

PaPa Jim McCormack designed record album covers and promoted many of the hit groups that he came in contact with during the 1960's. In the early '70s, his Chicago family began to vacation in Culver, and in 1976, he opened this restaurant at Lake Maxinkuckee. Today, the walls are filled with music-related memorabilia, reminding us of PaPa's interests so many years ago. Build your own pasta or create your own pizza. It's only fair to tell you that the pizza has been voted "Indiana's Best" by PaPa himself, obviously a great promoter! The menu also advertises some unique items: cheesecrisps, gazpacho martini soup, not skimpy shrimp, portabello pie, and stuffed spinach. Whether you are dining inside or out, you are surrounded by the lake atmosphere. PaPa's is truly a "Culver institution."

10. THE EDGEWATER GRILLE
620 Lakeshore Drive
Culver, IN 46511
(574) 842-2234
Open Tuesday-Sunday for lunch & dinner. Open Monday June, July, August.
Credit cards accepted.

With huge windows overlooking Lake Maxinkuckee, the Edgewater has quite a collection of marine memorabilia: boats hang from the ceiling, and surf boards, sailfish and paddles adorn the walls. Signs on display make you smile: "Maxinkuckee Mist --The Ale You Sailed On," "MAX WAX--surf board dressing AND hair pomade!" Booths in the bar with their own TVs have recently been added, along with private booths in the dining room. The menu is comprehensive, and you are sure to find your special favorite. The hot artichoke dip, jumbo coconut shrimp, wild mushroom ravioli, steak, or one of the nightly specials are all worth the trip. Appetizers include chips with peach salsa, jerk shrimp/chicken, quesadillas and cheese fries. Salad choices feature filet mignon or mahogany chicken with special dressings such as Thai peanut vinaigrette and ginger wasabi. There are hoagie and "odds and ends" sandwiches, "straw and hay" pasta, and pizza.

11. BACK FORTY JUNCTION
1011 North 13th Street
Decatur, IN 46733
(260) 724-3355
Open daily for lunch & dinner.
Credit cards accepted.

This establishment opened in the early 1950's and is "one big antique, from one end to the other," according to the manager. A restored caboose from circa 1800, along with a 1920's club car and many other railroad artifacts, sits outside. Tiffany lamps, as well as a lamp from Carole Lombard's home, light the interior. Burma Shave signs decorate the cathedral ceiling, and there are 15 John Rogers sculptures, depicting very detailed scenes of everyday American life in the 1800's, lining one wall. The buffet-style fare offers the traditional selections of steak, ribs and chicken, but the highlights are the prime rib carved daily and the all-you-can-eat crab legs on Friday nights.

12. FLYTRAPS

505 South Main Street
Elkhart, IN 46516
(574) 522-9328
Open Monday-Friday for lunch & dinner;
Saturday for dinner. Closed Sunday.
Credit cards accepted.

"Eat Well—Laugh Often—Live Long" is the invitation to those who choose to dine at this casual Main Street restaurant. A question you might be asking is why is a restaurant called Flytraps? Not to worry--the original owner of this almost 60-year-old establishment was nicknamed "Flytrap," and the present owners decided to stay with the same name! The atmosphere is very relaxed with photos of sunrises and sunsets decorating the walls. The specialty is fresh fish and most of the food is grilled. Lunch and dinner menus are printed daily, reflecting the freshest and healthiest food available with good taste always the goal. In addition to the fresh fish and seafood choices, the menu includes chicken, pasta, Black Angus beef, pork, and a wide range of nightly specials. There is an extensive wine list emphasizing the wines of California.

13. CATABLU

2441 Broadway
Fort Wayne, IN 46807
(260) 456-6563
Open Monday-Saturday for dinner. Closed Sunday.
Credit cards accepted.

This "gourmet American grill" is located in the old Indiana Theater, which dates back to 1923. The atmosphere is first class with original art adorning the walls and private dining on the upper level. The menu is filled with a wonderful selection of creatively prepared entrees that are visually enticing as well. Unique choices of smoked duck flatbread and sesame crusted calamari are offered for appetizers, followed by chop chop, apple or Caesar salads. Imaginative dinner entrees include black and blue cowboy steak with tabasco-fried onion rings, lobster mac 'n cheese, veal stuffed meatloaf and pesto rubbed mahi mahi. Wines, along with a full bar and many unique martinis, are available to complement each course.

14. CLUB SODA

235 East Superior Street
Fort Wayne, IN 46802
(260) 426-3442
Open Tuesday-Friday for lunch; Monday-Saturday for dinner.
Closed Sunday.
Credit cards accepted.

The old structure and brick walls of the Indiana Textile Company lend a lot of character to this upscale dining establishment. Dine on the main floor, the loft or, during warm weather, outdoors. There's live jazz on Friday and Saturday nights, and memorabilia from the original Rat Pack (Frank Sinatra, Sammy Davis, Jr. and Dean Martin) adorns the walls. The lunch menu features burgers, sandwiches, soups and salads. Dinner selections include Black Angus beef steak, prime rib, seafood, chicken, pork, duck, and two or three daily specials. There is an extensive martini menu, from the classics to "the dark side," and a large, diverse wine list. Call ahead for reservations, and you must be 21 to enter.

15. CONEY ISLAND WEINER STAND
131 West Main Street
Fort Wayne, IN 46802
(260) 424-2997
Open daily for lunch & dinner.
Cash only establishment.

Coney Island Weiner Stand could be considered a Fort Wayne historical landmark. Since 1914, people have been walking in and ordering hot dogs at the counter: 5, 10, and 20 at a time; with onions, coney sauce, and/or mustard; to eat in or take out! The buns are lined up, hot dogs inserted, extras added, then wrapped and boxed to go. Coke comes in 8-ounce glass bottles. If you eat "in," you can choose a stool at the counter or sit at the old porcelain topped tables. Historical photos of the restaurant and of Fort Wayne decorate the walls of this walk-in hot dog stand.

16. NINE MILE RESTAURANT
13398 U.S. Hwy 27 South
Fort Wayne, IN 46816
(260) 639-8112
Open Monday-Saturday for breakfast, lunch & dinner; Sunday for lunch & dinner.
Credit cards accepted.

A primitive tavern was established on this site in 1837, giving the Nine Mile Restaurant the right to advertise as the "oldest bar in Indiana!" Early settlers had good reason to stop at the Miller & King store and nearby tavern as they made their way across country. Today, there are very complete menus for all three meals. For breakfast, there are "Rise 'n Shine" sandwiches, home fries with gravy, cheezie eggs, and cinnamon and raisin toast. Lunch offers a variety of specialty sandwiches, salads and wraps. A comprehensive lunch and dinner menu features a variety of appetizers, soups, salads, specialty sandwiches and pizza, along with entrees of steak, baby back ribs, chicken and seafood. The restaurant prides itself in offering Waynedale Bakery pies for dessert. Full service catering is also available. Why is it called the Nine Mile Restaurant? Nine miles from what? Be sure to ask when you visit!

17. PAULA'S ON MAIN

1732 West Main Street
Fort Wayne, IN 46808
(260) 424-2300
Open Tuesday-Friday for lunch & dinner; Saturday for dinner.
Closed Sunday & Monday except for private parties.
Credit cards accepted.

This old factory building is a great setting for an upscale casual dining experience. Fish is the highlight, as you will note from the on-site fresh seafood market, the decor and the menu. With the market and the motif, it feels like you are eating at a restaurant down at the docks. The daily features, listed on a separate sheet, are highly recommended. In addition to seafood appetizers and salads, the lunch entrees include walleye, salmon, jambalaya, trout and whitefish. Additional offerings for dinner include entrees of grouper, cioppino (bouillabaisse), lake perch piccata and lobster. There is a "lighter side" section to the dinner menu, and chicken and steak selections if you're not in the mood for fish.

18. RIB ROOM

1235 East State Boulevard
Fort Wayne, IN 46805
(260) 483-9767
Open Monday-Friday for lunch & dinner; Saturday for dinner. Closed Sunday.
Credit cards accepted.

There is quite a history behind this restaurant, beginning many years ago with a partnership between the owners, Von Filippou and Nick Stamanis. It was originally named Nick's Rib Bar because Von, having immigrated from Greece, was not yet a U.S. citizen. Today, Von's son and son-in-law continue to maintain the Rib Room's reputation for good food, service and atmosphere. The menu has changed very little over the years, and they continue to serve thousands of pounds of ribs, french fries, baked potatoes and hash browns each week! In addition to their famous ribs, the menu includes sandwiches, salads and entrees for lunch, and steaks and seafood for dinner.

19. THE OYSTER BAR

1830 South Calhoun
Fort Wayne, IN 46802
(260) 744-9490
Open Monday-Friday for lunch & dinner; Saturday for dinner.
Closed Sunday.
Credit cards accepted.

A saloon that had been operating for 65 years was purchased in 1954 by Hughie Johnston, a local superstar athlete. He introduced oysters to the menu, but it wasn't until 1975 that the name became "The Oyster Bar." It feels like you have taken a step back in time as you view the photos of people who are long gone, sea memorabilia, and Fort Wayne historical pictures decorating the interior. The bar, which surrounds an old cooler, is wonderfully inviting and, in fact, customers sit on the stools and eat their meals. A blackboard behind the bar announces the daily specials like fisherman's stew, clam chowder, and pastrami and potato hash with poached eggs. Oysters can be prepared any way you want. Fresh fish can be flat grilled, oven roasted, cedar planked, pan sauteed or naked, which is oven-broiled in lemon butter. For non-seafood eaters there are options such as pork tenderloin, barbecued ribs, lamb and pecan chicken. A sign says seating capacity is 75, so reservations are suggested.

20. HERB GARDEN RESTAURANT
215 East State Road 120
Fremont, IN 46703
(260) 495-1658
Open Monday-Saturday for lunch & dinner. Closed Sunday.
Credit cards accepted.

Located near Pokagon State Park and just a half-mile east of the Horizon Outlet Mall, this charming restaurant is the perfect stop after a day at the park or when you need a break from shopping. Using the freshest ingredients available, the seasonal menu is filled with a tempting array of appetizers (try the yam fries or spinach balls for something different), specialty salads with homemade salad dressings, and a nice variety of sandwiches. Creatively prepared entrees feature seafood, chicken, beef, and pasta dishes, all very reasonably priced. Make sure you save room for dessert!

21. LAKE GEORGE RETREAT
35 Lane 110 A Lake George Drive
Fremont, IN 46703
(260) 833-2266
Open daily for dinner.
Credit cards accepted.

Watch the sun set over Lake George while eating your dinner. The appetizer menu offers shrimp prepared a number of ways: almond shrimp, coconut shrimp and shrimp cocktail. Entrees include salmon, raspberry chicken, and jambalaya. Salads with chicken or shrimp are also an option for your main course. Whatever you eat, you must save room for an item on the dessert tray! Lake George Retreat is a great place to enjoy a relaxing meal.

22. THE BLUEGILL
133 South Main Street
Goshen, IN 46526
(574) 534-4000
Open Tuesday-Friday for lunch; Monday-Saturday for dinner. Closed Sunday.
Credit cards accepted.

As you drive down the main street of Goshen, look for the blue awning with the artistically drawn fish--that's the Bluegill! Inside, you'll enjoy perusing the work of local area artists displayed on the brick walls while dining in a cozy, comfortable setting. Fresh seafood is featured daily, but steak, chicken, duck and pork are alternatives. The chef takes pride in developing a menu using seasonal ingredients and products from local markets. The crab cake is the signature item and appears on the menu as an entree for lunch and a starter for dinner. Other lunch possibilities include a ceviche tostada, penne pasta tossed with andouille sausage, and pulled pork. Halibut, walleye and scallops mixed with fresh ingredients and special sauces highlight the dinner menu. For the lighter appetite, there are smaller portions of many items.

23. PIER 32
6665 State Road 1
Hamilton Lake, IN 46742
(260) 488-2808
Open daily for lunch & dinner. Closed Mondays in winter.
Credit cards accepted.

Escape to the lake and enjoy a meal on the porch overlooking the dock or from inside overlooking the water. From either vantage point, Pier 32 offers good food in a care-free, vacation-like atmosphere where the message over the fireplace in the bar reads: "No time is wasted making a friend." Cleverly named appetizers can be enjoyed with one of the specialty beers: Northwoods Brie (maple plank grilled brie with Vermont syrup), Wrigley Field (ballpark pretzels with spicy mustard sauce), and Boneless in Buffalo (skewered chicken and vegetables with buffalo sauce), to name a few. For lunch, there are wraps, pitas, croissants, frog legs, pesto linguini, soups and salads. The dinner menu features selections from the sea, fresh water, Walla Walla (lamb sausage, Vidalia onion and apple), Carolina Smokehouse (ribs), American Chop House (steak, lamb, pork), and Down on the Bayou or Rocky Mountain High (chicken).

24. PHIL SMIDT & SON
1205 North Calumet Avenue
Hammond, IN 46320
(219) 659-0025; (800) 376-4534
Open Tuesday-Sunday for lunch & dinner. Closed Monday.
Credit cards accepted.

From its humble beginnings in 1910 as a dining room with three tables, twelve seats, a twelve-foot bar and attached boat livery to its notoriety today as a world famous restaurant, Phil Smidt's continues to maintain its reputation for quality food and ser-vice. The frog legs and lake perch, deep fried or sauteed, are the stars of the menu. You'll also enjoy the traditional choices of steaks, chicken and seafood, along with surf and turf combos, walleyed pike, baked salmon, and shrimp served in several guises. Your dining experience won't be complete, however, until you try one of the "berried" treasures: blackberry, gooseberry or black raspberry pie!

25. THE BREAD BASKET
7205 Indianapolis Boulevard
Hammond, IN 46324
(219) 845-7890
Open Tuesday-Saturday for lunch. Closed Sunday & Monday.
Credit cards accepted.

Inspired by their west coast roots, The Bread Basket is a family owned and operated delicatessen and café that features "Homemade goodness for your goodness." From the menu to the decor, The Bread Basket was designed to function as an extension of the family home. The cuisine is structured around the legendary homemade bread of several varieties used to make delicious sandwiches. Taste-tempting soups and salads are also on the menu. All recipes are original creations gleaned from family recipes and travels from Seattle to New York. Signature dishes include almond chicken, grilled panini sandwiches and baked potato soup. Specialty non-alcoholic drinks are available, made with coffee, fruit juice, ice cream and yogurt. Top off the meal with a sweet treat: carrot cake, caramel bars or pound cake. You can also take home a fresh baked loaf of bread after your meal!

26. MARTI'S PLACE at RAMSEY'S LANDING
17519 North 700 West
Hebron, IN 46341
(219) 996-3363
Open daily for lunch & dinner.
Credit cards accepted.

Nestled on the scenic wooded banks of the Kankakee River, you can dine in a relaxed setting while enjoying a wonderful view of the river, birds, and landscape--an "in the country, away from the noise and hub-bub" experience! A mouth-watering selection of seafood is available: shrimp coconut, red fish (blazing or mild), walleye, catfish, lake perch, and frog leg saddles. For meat and poultry fans, there are St. Louis ribs, pork chops, prime rib and chicken choices. Sandwiches and munchies are served for lunch. The health-conscious diner will appreciate the fact that Marti's uses Breakthrough Products, and the menu contains information about calories, fat and fiber.

27. COUNTRY LOUNGE
3700 Montgomery
Hobart, IN 46342
(219) 942-6699
Open daily for lunch & dinner.
Credit cards accepted.

Friendly conversation between the tables and at the bar lets you know that this is a local gathering place. The restaurant has been in existence for over 70 years, and even though the name has changed several times, it still maintains the same traditions of "good food, good value, and fine service in a congenial atmosphere." Caricatures of customers line the bar room walls, reportedly sketched by a person "who is now in heaven." The lounge has the nickname "Hunkee Hollow," based on its popularity with the European immigrants who love home cooking with emphasis on good, natural flavor rather than reliance on heavy spices. Luncheon specials often reflect the recipes from Poland, Yugoslavia, Hungary and Romania. Lake perch, the house specialty, is the most popular dish and it fulfills the expectation. A well-rounded lunch and dinner menu also includes salads, sandwiches, steak, chops and chicken entrees, plus seafood and combination platters. This is a great place to stop on the way to and from Chicago.

28. DILLINGER'S

302 Main Street
Hudson, IN 46747
(260) 587-3377
Open daily for lunch & dinner. (Call for winter hours.)
Credit cards accepted.

The old corner Hudson Bank--the bank that Dillinger's gang reportedly robbed in 1933--houses this out-of-the-way restaurant. The old safe is the focal point in the bar and the walls tell the story of Dillinger's activities in 1933 and 1934. Placemats on the tables are created from newspaper articles, offering interesting reading while waiting for your meal! The lunch menu plays on the names of gangsters: Dillinger white chili, Scarface chef salad, Babyface Nelson burger, Ma Barker BLT, and Capone Club. The dinner menu offers steaks, chops, chicken, ribs and seafood. A salad bar is available with entrees on Friday and Saturday.

29. NICK'S KITCHEN

506 North Jefferson
Huntington, IN 46750
(260) 356-6618
Open Monday-Saturday for breakfast & lunch. Closed Sunday.
Credit cards accepted.

In the morning or at lunchtime, Nick's proclaims, "We don't do fast food. We just do great food fast!" Dan Quayle's hometown campaign visits made people throughout the state aware of Nick's and the famous breaded tenderloin that "you need both hands to eat!" Pictures on the walls of this local downtown diner verify Quayle's visits, in addition to historic photos of the town and the trains that stopped at the station. A breakfast bowl with eggs, potatoes, bacon, and sausage gravy that you eat with a spoon is a popular breakfast choice. Of course, there are scrams, cheesy potatoes and Ossian bone-in ham. For lunch, there's the "original" breaded tenderloin mentioned above or a Quayle burger with fries, plus hand-dipped shakes and fresh baked pies. You'll enjoy "people-watching" as the local citizens sit around listening to the morning news or gather around the long "community" table, complete with atlases and dictionaries to settle friendly disagreements about the facts!

30. GAMBA RISTORANTE

455 East 84th Drive
Merrillville, IN 46140
(219) 736-5000
Open Monday-Saturday for lunch & dinner. Closed Sunday.
Credit cards accepted.

A favorite stop when traveling to or from Chicago has changed its name and location, but the food continues to be uniquely wonderful Northern Italian. As you enter Gamba's, circular patterns catch your eye: the globe chandeliers, the alcoves, the glasses, the rooms. While the atmosphere is upscale, it is as comfortable and inviting as their slogan suggests: "Where Family Becomes Family." The seasonal menu offers five courses (antipasti, zuppe, insalata, paste, secondi) plus dessert. Dishes are presented with their Italian names and then described in mouth-watering terms, such as Croquette Di Granchi, crab cake with spicy orange mayo and tomato apricot chutney, and Raviolini Prelibati, handcrafted ravioli filled with sausage, ricotta, and plum tomato sauce. The lunch menu is not simply smaller portions of items on the dinner menu, but additional choices in each of the five courses. You can eat lunch on your way to Chicago and dinner on your way home and have completely different taste experiences.

31. MAXINE'S RESTAURANT & BAR
521 Franklin Street
Michigan City, IN 46360
(219) 872-4500
Open daily for dinner.
Credit cards accepted.

Years ago, while traveling back and forth from Michigan to Indiana, the present owner would stop at his favorite restaurant in Michigan City, originally named Maxine & Heine's. When the opportunity arose for him to take over the establishment, he decided to honor the past and rename the restaurant Maxine's. The interior has been enhanced with a full wall mural of a scene of life in France. The menu offers a nice selection of entrees prepared in the open kitchen. You may choose the daily dinner special or order from the menu: steak, lamb, veal, venison, chicken or seafood. Pasta and ravioli are made daily, the signature dish being Vincigrasi Santa Maria, a lasagna recipe from southern Italy.

32. PUMPS ON 12
3085 West Dunes Highway 12
Michigan City, IN 46360
(219) 874-6201
Open daily for lunch & dinner.
Credit cards accepted.

Are you planning to spend a day at the Dunes? Don't bother packing a lunch because Pumps on 12 is a fun and reasonably priced place to stop, as well as a great spot for dinner on your way home. As the name implies, it was once a place to fill the gas tank and the memorabilia inside reminds you of the old-fashioned filling stations of days gone by. The menu carries out the theme as well: Water Pumps (seafood entrees), regular, premium, or unleaded pizza, Pink Cadillac chicken salad, Pump burgers, and Roadster Ribeye.

33. RODINI'S RESTAURANT

4125 Franklin Street
Michigan City, IN 46360
(219) 879-7388
Open Monday-Friday for lunch & dinner; Saturday & Sunday for dinner.
Credit cards accepted.

"Rodini" is a valley in Rhodes, one of the most beautiful islands in Greece and the owner Larry's home. In keeping with his roots, Rodini's in Michigan City has been offering unique tastes of Greece--and a whole lot more--for over 35 years. The restaurant is located in a very nondescript area and building, but once inside you will be more than pleasantly surprised by the food and the atmosphere. Try the Greek-style pork chops, Rodini's seasoned rack of lamb, or the chef's special of beef tenderloin, green peppers, onions and mushrooms, smothered with fried tomatoes. Cajun scallops, fresh lake perch, shrimp, and frog legs are also on the menu in this highly acclaimed establishment.

34. SWINGBELLY'S

100 Washington Street
Michigan City, IN 46360
(219) 874-5718
Open daily for lunch & dinner.
Credit cards accepted.

Whether you are in Michigan City to visit the outlet mall or the beautiful sandy beach, this is a great place to stop and enjoy a meal. Head for Lake Michigan and look for the railroad station next to the tracks. The station has been well-maintained with original lights and polished wood floors. While you eat, you can watch boats coming and going in Washington Park. Hand-pattied burgers are what they claim to do best, but there's a wide range of sandwiches, clubs and subs for lunch. Dinner includes steaks, chops, shrimp, lake perch, and chicken among the many offerings.

35. DAS DUTCHMAN ESSENHAUS

240 US 20
Middlebury, IN 46540
(574) 825-9471; (800) 455-9471
Open Monday-Saturday for breakfast, lunch & dinner.
Closed Sunday.
Credit cards accepted.

Located in the heart of Amish country, you will find this restaurant and the surrounding village to be a pleasant surprise. Depending on your appetite, you can choose either a la carte or family style meals with generous helpings made from scratch "the old fashioned way." Family style dinners are all-you-can-eat featuring salad, broasted chicken and a choice of roast beef, ham or baked steak, plus Amish dressing, mashed potatoes, corn and homemade noodles. Your meal is not complete without the homemade bread and apple butter, plus a variety of delectable desserts: tapioca or date pudding, warm apple dumpling, or a slice of homemade pie. The on-site bakery also offers treats to take home. If you would like to stay and enjoy the area, there's a variety of activities for the whole family: shops, an animal farm with other attractions for children, and miniature golf nearby.

36. MILLER BAKERY CAFÉ
555 South Lake Street
Miller Beach (Gary), IN 46403
(219) 938-2229
Open Tuesday-Friday for lunch & dinner;
Saturday & Sunday for dinner. Closed Monday.
Credit cards accepted.

As you approach the landmark Miller Bakery, built in 1941, the old storefront is no indication of what you'll find inside! Open the door and you are treated to an exciting array of colors, from the wood floors to the creamy marble and burgundy walls. High ceilings with exposed duct work and tables covered with paper and crayons add to the atmosphere, along with some of the original pastry cabinets on display. Background music varies from Billie Holliday to New-Age on any given day. The lunch and dinner menus specialize in a global cuisine that changes with the seasons, featuring items such as fresh Thai salmon filet, midwestern pork chops, Indiana duck breast, and sea scallops with corn and shittake mushrooms.

37. MAURY'S PAT'S PUB
901 West 4th Street
Mishawaka, IN 46544
(574) 259-8282
Open Monday-Friday for lunch & dinner; Saturday for dinner. Closed Sunday.
Credit cards accepted.

From the outside, the pub looks like a non-descript neighborhood corner bar with the year 1910 carved on the building and an awning over the steps leading to the door. However, one step inside tells you a different story! Your eyes are drawn to the crisp white tablecloths, and then to the Notre Dame memorabilia covering the walls. A chandelier that is actually a basketball net holding a basketball hangs from the ceiling, and light bulbs flash with the playing of the Notre Dame fight song. A dog sled is also suspended from the ceiling, which is explained by the Iditarod dog race pictures and articles on the back wall. (The owner sponsors an Iditarod team.) In addition to the signature pork chops available every evening, patrons frequent the restaurant for the daily specials: Monday--kabobs, prime rib and pork; Tuesday--spaghetti with homemade sauce; Wednesday--BBQ ribs; Thursday--chicken and pork; Friday--shrimp de jonghe and prime rib; Saturday--prime rib. Fresh fish and lake perch are also big sellers, along with steaks served in a variety of ways: seasoned, marinated, blackened, peppered, or smothered. On the lighter side, you'll find a nice variety of homemade soups and salads and, after 10:00 pm, a sandwich menu.

38. PAPA JOE'S CASA DE PASTA
1209 South Union
Mishawaka, IN 46544
(574) 255-0890
Open Friday & Saturday for dinner.
Credit cards accepted.

You'll smile as you enter this restaurant and notice the upside down umbrellas and plants hanging from the ceiling! Twinkling lights reflect on the wood tables and highlight the warm red accents in every nook and cranny of the dining area. When preparing to open the restaurant in 1973, the owner searched for a specialty to offer patrons and was reminded of the homemade pastas created by her mother. Today, the spaghetti is imported from Italy and the menu is filled with mouth-watering combinations of vegetables, meats, pasta and sauces. A family owned operation, several items on the menu carry the names of family members.

39. CAFÉ ELISE
435 Ridge Road
Munster, IN 46321
(219) 836-2233
Open Tuesday-Friday for lunch; Tuesday-Sunday for dinner.
Closed Monday.
Credit cards accepted.

The restaurant advertises "unique presentations" and that statement applies in several ways. It is located in a barely recognizable strip of shops, but when you open the door, you are enchanted by the artistically eclectic decor: chairs with flowered upholstery, china plates of different patterns, and art on the walls. The restaurant's logo incorporates the likeness of the owner's daughter, Elise. The food is unique and wonderful. Highlights include the bread and special butter, roasted beet salad, Merlot poached pears, chicken carbonara, crab cakes, sweet potato ravioli, and wood-roasted chicken. Bread pudding and other homemade desserts are truly worthy of saving room. You'll appreciate the "unique presentation" on your plate as well!

40. GIOVANNI'S
603 Ridge Road
Munster, IN 46321
(219) 836-6220
Open Monday-Friday for lunch & dinner; Saturday for dinner.
Closed Sunday.
Credit cards accepted.

Procopio LoDuca immigrated to the United States as a young boy and achieved his dream of opening a small pizza restaurant at this location in 1966. Later, he enlarged and remodeled to become the Giovanni's of today, still family owned and operated. One specialty is the "Nothing BeatZZA" pizza, but the chef's crab cakes, fried artichoke, seafood risotto, hand-made ravioli, veal rollatini, and grilled pork medallions are mouth-watering alternatives. You must also consider the daily specials, decided upon early in the morning based on the best available ingredients in the market that day. When asked, "What is a really good 'Dining Secrets' restaurant in northern Indiana?," many people responded with Giovanni's at the top of their list. Customer service is of utmost importance to the staff, which is quite evident when you dine here.

41. WAGNER'S RIBS
361 Wagner Road
Porter, IN 46304
(219) 926-7614
Open daily for lunch & dinner.
Credit cards accepted.

After a long day at the dunes, stop by Wagner's for ribs: baby back, spare or country style. They bottle their own tasty sauce and you can purchase some to take home. Sides of waffle fries, onion rings, coleslaw and corn bread cakes are choices to go with the entrees which, in addition to the ribs, include steak, chicken, pork, pollack and perch. If you prefer a sandwich, choose from fish'n chips, Italian dip and burgers. Eli's cheesecakes are a delightful way to top off your meal. Wagner's has beer signs on the walls, labels on the tables, and serves many of the mentioned beers. You must be 21 to enter this country bar.

42. CITY OFFICE & PUB
114 South Van Rensselaer Street
Rensselaer, IN 47978
(219) 866-9916
Open Tuesday-Saturday for lunch & dinner. Closed Sunday & Monday.
Credit cards accepted.

As the county seat, Rensselaer needed a convenient eating spot so the City Pub opened to fill that void. In the process of renovating the space that used to be a pharmacy, signs of the original design and decor were uncovered, including restaurant booths and brick-tile inlaid archways. The antique atmosphere has been maintained, creating a comfortable setting for both locals and visitors. A collage of old courthouses and other antique pictures decorate the walls. Additional seating is available at the bar or on the elevated porch. Steaks are the specialty, but prime rib, pan-fried lake perch, barbecued ribs and chicken wings are other popular choices.

43. SOLLY'S
Highway 24
Reynolds, IN 47980
(219) 984-5512
Open Tuesday-Saturday for dinner. Closed Sunday & Monday.
Credit cards accepted.

The original owner of Solly's, Mr. Solomon, spent 42 years building "a steak house, pure and simple, no fancy adjectives." Even though he no longer owns the business, his traditions continue. The present owners are also committed to hand-cutting the meats, grinding their own hamburger, and tossing the salad with Solly's famous red arrow dressing. In keeping with the Southwestern decor, you will find a totem pole outside and an Indian arrow over the fireplace. Choice aged steaks are the house specialty, but chicken and catfish are also popular items.

44. JOSEPH DECUIS

191 North Main Street
Roanoke, IN 46783
(260) 672-1715
Open Tuesday-Saturday for lunch & dinner. Closed Sunday & Monday.
Credit cards accepted.

You may not be familiar with Roanoke, but be assured that one of the most memorable dining experiences awaits you in this small Indiana town! The ambiance is of Old World luxury and comfort with each room offering a different venue. Club Creole is a formal dining room and bar located in the historic Roanoke State Bank building. Two original bank vaults house the walk-in cigar humidor and nationally-acclaimed wine cellar. Cafe Creole is the entrance dining room and features the exhibition kitchen where you can watch the culinary artists at work. A Victorian conservatory offers dining in tropical elegance, and an outdoor New Orleans-style courtyard is surrounded by beautifully landscaped gardens. The surroundings are not the only story. The cuisine is "gourmet dining in the Creole tradition"...an imaginative blend of classical cooking, unique ingredients and artful presentation. Lunch menus are revised quarterly and reflect seasonal fare in a variety of salads, sandwiches, special entrees and desserts. The dinner menu changes weekly to feature the finest and freshest ingredients and allows for the chef's creativity. A "typical" dinner selection might include a Caribbean seafood cocktail appetizer, hoisin duck salad, and an entree of pan sautéed Dover sole or a fresh herb-crusted rack of lamb. It is a treat to the tastebuds to merely read the menu! Be sure to look at the Tim Johnson oil paintings and sculptures. Jazz music is featured on weekends.

45. ROANOKE VILLAGE INN

190 Main (Off US 24 West)
Roanoke, IN 46783
(260) 672-3707
Open Monday-Saturday for lunch & dinner. Closed Sunday.
Cash or checks accepted.

Simply "a bar with great food" is how this full service bar and restaurant was described by a Huntington resident. They are best known for both the broiled and deep fried haddock, deep fried butterflied shrimp, and the popular 16 ounce barbecued pork chop. Additional choices include barbecued ribs, a full line of steaks, and chicken entrees.

46. TEIBEL'S RESTAURANT

1775 US Highway 41 (US 30 & 41)
Schererville, IN 46375
(219) 865-2000
Open daily for lunch & dinner.
Credit cards accepted.

Teibel's first opened its doors in 1929 and has operated continuously ever since. Customers come here for the delicious chicken and lake perch that have made Teibel's famous throughout the area. In fact, the family who submitted this recommendation said they have yet to find any other place where lake perch can compare to Teibel's. Banquet facilities are also available for business meetings or any occasion. Call for banquet menu information.

47. BLUE GATE RESTAURANT

195 North Van Buren
Shipshewana, IN 46565
(260) 768-4725
Open Monday-Saturday for breakfast, lunch & dinner.
Closed Sunday.
Credit cards accepted.

Plan to spend the day at the Riegsecker Marketplace where you can shop for your favorite collectibles, enjoy an old-fashioned buggy ride, tour the furniture and model horse factories, and have a relaxing meal at the Blue Gate Restaurant. You will enjoy the traditional Amish/Mennonite-style cooking, made from scratch, served off the menu or family-style by Amish and Mennonite waitresses. Treat yourself to a hearty country breakfast from a variety of choices. The lunch and dinner menus include a nice selection of salads and sandwiches, along with their most popular menu items: chicken, ham, and roast beef served with mashed potatoes, gravy, dressing, vegetable, salad, and homemade bread. If possible, you must save room for the delectable desserts or take one home from the bakery!

48. CARRIAGE HOUSE

Corner of Orange & Adams Roads
South Bend, IN 46628
(574) 272-9220
Open Tuesday-Saturday for dinner. Closed Sunday & Monday.
Credit cards accepted.

Built in 1851 as a Brethren church emphasizing the simplistic, it is difficult to imagine this history as you step inside the elegantly appointed restaurant occupying the space today. Along with classical music in the background, the traditional antiques and tastefully selected accessories decorating the interior provide a most pleasant environment for this fine dining experience. Begin the meal with a choice of cold or warm appetizers: steak tartare, smoked salmon, Mediterranean grape leaves or rabbit sausage. Outstanding entrees include Beef Wellington, rack of lamb, steaks, veal and seafood. As recipients of the Wine Spectator "Best" Award, you can be assured of an extensive wine list. Excellence is clearly the goal here.

49. LASALLE GRILL
115 West Colfax Avenue
South Bend, IN 46601
(574) 288-1155; (800) 382-9323
Open Monday-Saturday for dinner. Closed Sundays.
Credit cards accepted.

LaSalle Grill has a well-deserved reputation for providing guests with a memorable dining experience in a lively, upscale atmosphere, unlike any other in the area. The cuisine is modern American, a blend of many classic and ethnic ingredients using only the highest quality and freshest foods available. Items change daily to reflect the seasons and are designed to stimulate and intrigue the palate; the presentation is unique and creative. In addition to a superb selection of appetizers, desserts and an award-winning wine list, there is an outstanding choice of entrees: rack of New Zealand lamb, pan-crisp breast of Indiana duckling, and their own dry aged prime steaks cooked over a live, hardwood fire. You can also enjoy the menu Tuesday through Saturday in the lounge, Club LaSalle, where you will find an entertainment venue unique to South Bend featuring classic cocktails, stylish decor, and live music.

50. TIPPECANOE PLACE
620 West Washington
South Bend, IN 46601
(574) 234-9077
Open Monday-Friday for lunch & dinner;
Saturday for dinner; Sunday for brunch & dinner.
Credit cards accepted.

This elegant mansion, the original home built by the Studebaker family in 1888, is the embodiment of everything great wealth in the 1880's could suggest. Its four levels of exquisite architecture and detailing, including 40 rooms and 20 fireplaces, provided a magnificent backdrop for many lavish parties, weddings and balls that were prized invitations by South Bend society. Today, Tippecanoe Place is still known for its hospitality and as a gracious setting for fine dining. With the exception of the addition of a modern kitchen and bar, great attention has been paid to preserving the original atmosphere of these grand rooms that are now the dining areas. Its award-winning fare includes a wonderful variety of appetizers, entrees, and desserts created daily by their pastry chef. The house specialty is "perfect" prime rib. Sunday brunch is a veritable feast, offering a wide variety of appealing selections. Reservations are recommended.

51. OAKWOOD INN

849 East Lake View Road
(Hidden entrance, 1 1/2 blocks off Highway 13)
Syracuse, IN 46567
(574) 457-5600
Open Tuesday-Saturday for lunch & dinner; Sunday for breakfast & brunch.
Closed Monday.
Credit cards accepted.

Escape to this retreat center owned by the Oakwood Foundation for Adult Christian Ministries, Inc. Located on 40 acres on Lake Wawasee, the largest natural lake in northern Indiana, the beautifully appointed oak structure that houses the hotel/ restaurant and the surrounding grounds are designed to provide an environment for peaceful reflection. Enjoy dining in a relaxed setting with a wall of windows over- looking the lake. A full service, moderately priced menu specializing in fresh fish, prime rib, steak, pasta and stir fry is complemented by wonderful pastries prepared by the chef on premises. Weekends feature a fish fry buffet on Friday and prime rib buffet on Saturday. (Smoke-free environment; no alcohol served.)

52. SLEEPY OWL SUPPER CLUB

11374 North State Road 13
Syracuse, IN 46567
(574) 457-4840
Open daily for lunch & dinner.
Credit cards accepted.

There's a sleepy owl on a branch over the door but lots of activity inside! The menu lists many familiar choices packaged in a different way, such as armadillo eggs (stuffed jalepeno peppers) and foot o'rings (onion rings with warrior sauce). The "Pasta Picks" are Italian dishes from the recipes of the owner's grandmother. The home- made breaded tenderloin made the Sleepy Owl famous--it is so big, it won't fit in the bun! An "endless bowl of salad" accompanies the entrees of steak, chicken, pork chops, and the popular barbecued ribs. The "World's Smallest Sundae" for 50 cents is a "sweet ending."

53. BISTRO 157

157 West Lincolnway
Valparaiso, IN 46383
(219) 462-0992
Open Tuesday-Friday for lunch; Tuesday-Sunday for dinner. Closed Monday.
Credit cards accepted.

Nestled among the stores in downtown Valparaiso is a jewel of a restaurant. The walls are brick, the art is modern, the atmosphere is eclectic, and the chef/owner, Nicole Bissonnette, is very talented. Having received her culinary training in France, she found that patrons were a little unsure of the creativity of her menus at first. But now, the seared foie gras "liver and onions" presentation, Mediterranean calamari salad and shellfish paella are accepted and enjoyed. For the less adventurous, crab cakes might be a first course choice, followed by beef tenderloin or chicken with penne pasta. There is also a vegetarian whim for your consideration. In nice weath- er, you can dine at a table outside on the sidewalk.

54. BON FEMME CAFE
66 West Lincolnway
Valparaiso, IN 46383
(219) 531-0612
Open daily for lunch & dinner.
Credit cards accepted.

As you walk into the restaurant, a mural of a woman drinking a glass of wine stands out. Perhaps this is the reason for the name "Bon Femme." However, the name of this establishment could also be Bon Nourriture (good food, nourishment). The cuisine is American with a French accent, which means creativity in taste and presentation. For instance, a lunch sandwich is called Croque Monsieur (Crunchy Mister) and has smoked ham, port salut cheese and Dijon mustard on grilled homemade bread; the Croque Madam adds a fried egg. Steaks are at the top of the dinner menu, but options are sauteed grouper with a "kiss of wine," and vegetarian risotto. Bread pudding is the signature dessert, but raspberry truffles and banana Foster crepes may tempt you to be really sinful! Friday and Saturday evenings feature live entertainment.

55. DISH RESTAURANT
3907 North Calumet
Valparaiso, IN 46383
(219) 465-9221
Open Monday-Friday for lunch & dinner; Saturday for dinner. Closed Sunday.
Credit cards accepted.

Dishes hang from the walls and ceiling in this friendly, upscale restaurant. The creative menu changes every three months, featuring main courses and comfort foods for dinner. You should hope that the gorgonzola potato chips, oven roasted beet salad, and sesame chicken breast appear on the menu! There is also homemade spaetzle, merlot-braised short ribs, and lots of other delicious entrees and specials. In addition to salads and sandwiches, the lunch menu includes many of the dinner and pasta choices with some wonderful additions like baked macaroni and cheese with ham. You can see all of the yummy-looking orders coming from the open kitchen! There is also a full-service bar.

56. RESTAURANTE DON QUIJOTE
119 East Lincolnway
Valparaiso, IN 46383
(219) 462-7976
Open Monday-Friday for lunch & dinner; Saturday for dinner.
Closed Sunday.
Credit cards accepted.

Advertised as the first Spanish restaurant in Indiana, the chef/owner introduces patrons to authentic Spanish cooking. The food is carefully prepared from natural ingredients, emphasizing classic regional cuisines of Spain which he clearly states "are not fast food." Over twenty choices of tapas (appetizers) are offered, including shrimp, grilled or sauteed, Spanish style meatballs, cured Spanish ham, and potatoes in a spicy sauce, followed by sopas (gazpacho or soup of the day) and four varieties of ensalada (salad). Then, get ready for the comidas (dinners)! A specialty of the house is Paella, either Marinera or Valenciana. Other wonderful choices are marinated grilled pork loin with roasted red peppers, roasted lamb stuffed with green olives, Trucha a la Navarra (trout), and Bacalao a la Vasca (cod). All of these tempting selections can be enjoyed in surroundings that look and feel like a Spanish cafe.

57. STRONGBOW TURKEY INN
Junction of State Road 49 & US 30
Valparaiso, IN 46383
(219) 462-5121; (800) 462-5121
Open daily for lunch & dinner.
Credit cards accepted.

Now in its third generation of family ownership, the restaurant was named after the Potawatomi Indian chief who lived on the land with his tribe in the 19th century. The grandparents of the present owners began raising their first crop of turkeys in 1937. In 1940, both US Highway 30 and the Inn opened simultaneously with a 28-seat dining room, eight cabins for overnight guests and three gas pumps. It has steadily grown over the years into the complex it is today with public and private dining rooms, a cocktail lounge, bakery, and a premier banquet and convention center accommodating up to 500 guests. Strongbow offers sandwiches and salads for lunch and beef and seafood selections for dinner, but obviously turkey dishes are their signature items. The traditional turkey dinner, famous turkey pie, and adaptations of other dishes, such as turkey schnitzel and turkey oskar, are wonderful. "One of the finest examples of Hoosier hospitality and fine dining."

58. MARKET STREET GRILL
90 West Market
Wabash, IN 46992
(260) 563-7779
Open Tuesday-Friday for lunch & dinner; Saturday for dinner.
Closed Sunday & Monday.
Credit cards accepted.

The interior of this restaurant reflects the owner's interest in trains and antiques. Lots of memorabilia covers the brick walls and creates a backdrop for the electric train that travels throughout the restaurant. You can enjoy a drink or a bottle of beer delivered in an ice bucket while waiting in one of the old barber chairs! Begin your meal with bacon, lettuce and tomato soup, followed by one of the house specialties: "drunk'in chicken" or barbecued ribs. In addition to steaks and seafood, the menu offers a nice selection of low fat entrees, sandwiches, and their award-winning chili. Monthly specials are offered as well. You must be 21 to enter. Consistently voted "Best All Around Restaurant, Steak and Caterer in Wabash County."

59. CERULEAN RESTAURANT & SUSHI LOUNGE

1100 East Canal Street
Winona Lake, IN 46590
(574) 269-1226
Open Monday-Saturday for lunch & dinner. Closed Sunday.
Credit cards accepted.

While in the Northern Indiana lake region, you will enjoy visiting this restaurant for both the food and the atmosphere. You can dine on the porch overlooking the canal or eat inside in a sophisticated, well-appointed dining room where the decor entertains you with its colors and shapes. The menu offers significant choices. Japanese Bento Boxes are the lunch attraction: you select one main item like honey panko crusted chicken, spicy lemon shrimp, soft shell crab or tempura vegetable; then you choose three sides such as Asian noodles, field green salad, or edamame. For dinner, there's a list of mouth-watering tapas: basil-lime drizzled shrimp with olives, chicken skewers with capers and sauce, and honey-balsamic pork with seared strawberries. In addition, there are pasta dishes, meat and vegetarian choices, salads and soups. A complete menu of sushi, sashimi, maki rolls and chef specialty rolls is always available. Of course, the desserts are excellent, too. Pavlova, a fresh fruit pie with a meringue crust, is superb!

60. BILLY'S

18000 Lincoln Highway East
Zulu (Monroeville), IN 46773
(260) 623-3583
Open Tuesday-Sunday for dinner. Closed Monday.
Credit cards accepted.

Tell your friends you would like to take them to dinner at a bar in downtown Zulu, Indiana. Yes, when naming the town, a globe was spun around and the finger landed on Zulu in Africa. Plaid booths, a statue of the Blues Brothers, a juke box, sports memorabilia, and the "Wall of Shame or is it Fame" with its collages of regular customers all combine to create an inviting atmosphere. Popular menu items include the broiled or fried haddock, filet, T-bone and pork chops, or you may prefer the Mexican food choices of nachos, burritos or flautas. This is a bar, and smoking is permitted.

Central Indiana

61. FLETCHER'S OF ATLANTA
185 West Main Street
Atlanta, IN 46031
(765) 292-2777
Open Tuesday-Saturday for dinner. Closed Sunday & Monday.
Credit cards accepted.

This peaceful, small town restaurant is just a short drive from Indianapolis and certainly worth the trip. The white walls are decorated with paintings by Hoosier artists, and a relaxed atmosphere sets the stage for "contemporary Hoosier eclectic dining," meaning food prepared by Indiana chefs with Indiana ingredients. The menu features beef, chicken, pork, pastas, and daily fresh fish specials. One person said the following about Fletcher's: "Great fresh seafood in the midst of the cornfields. When available, the sea bass is as good as you'll find this side of Coronado Island."

62. CINNAMON ROOSTER
7900 East US 36
Avon, IN 46123
(317) 272-7332
Open Tuesday-Saturday for breakfast & lunch;
Sunday for breakfast only. Closed Monday.
Credit cards accepted.

Order the "Colossal" and you'll get a cinnamon roll the size of a 12-inch pizza! Fortunately, a slice is also available. To accompany the slice, there are omelettes, quiche and just ordinary eggs with bacon, ham or sausage and "arpotatoes." Hay Bales (biscuits and gravy), Silos (pancakes), Utmost Bagel, waffles and French toast are also great breakfast choices. For lunch, sandwiches like the Turkey Strut, BBQ of the day (beef, pork or chicken) and Tuscan (lamb) are served with sides of cucumbers and onions, river beans, cole slaw or potato salad. Soups, salads and daily specials are also offered. An occasional rooster can be seen in this pleasantly bright and airy restaurant where tables and booths invite customers to sit, visit, and enjoy a meal.

63. NAPOLI VILLA
758 Main Street
Beech Grove, IN 46107
(317) 783-4122
Open Monday-Friday for lunch & dinner; Saturday for dinner. Closed Sunday.
Credit cards accepted.

Napoli Villa first opened its doors in 1962 to Italian immigrants. Today, the same family operates the restaurant, continuing the traditions that made this trattoria so popular. Upon entering the restaurant, the old world aromas of the fresh tomato sauce send you back to Italy. There's a nice variety of pastas, pizzas and sandwiches. For the more adventurous, a wide range of gourmet dishes are offered, such as the Gambarella (shrimp) alla Romana and Pollo alla Cacciatore. Don't forget to save room for dolce: a mouth-watering selection of traditional and contemporary desserts.

64. BOGGSTOWN CABARET

6895 West Boggstown Road
Boggstown, IN 46110
(317) 835-2020; (800) 672-2656
Open daily. Luncheon & dinner shows.
Reservations required.
Credit cards accepted.

Since the early 1980's, the Boggstown Cabaret has been providing the very best in fresh, delicious food and live musical entertainment. It is located 20 miles southeast of Indianapolis between Greenwood and Shelbyville, just five miles from the horse racing park. The Cabaret delights audiences with a professional, interactive, fast-paced show. Combining original ideas and music from the 1920's to present, it is the place to go for pure unadulterated laughter. The unique menu is filled with items you'll love that are "made fresh to order." Try a fresh, piping hot fried biscuit and the mouthwatering freshly battered walleye. Package pricing includes show, dinner, dessert, beverage, tax and gratuity.

65. TOP NOTCH BAR & GRILL

113 South 3rd Street
Brookston, IN 47923
(765) 563-6508
Open Monday-Thursday for lunch & dinner;
Friday & Saturday for dinner. Closed Sunday.
Cash or checks accepted.

Come with a big appetite on Friday and Saturday nights for excellent steaks, including "the best filet mignon you will ever eat at a price you can't beat!" Also, be prepared to share a good joke with Bob, the bartender, who is a walking joke book and is guaranteed to entertain you. The atmosphere is casual and friendly, and the long lines are worth the wait.

66. RILEYBROOK HALL

Brookville, IN 47012
(800) 406-5169
Call for reservations.
Open Tuesday-Thursday for lunch;
Friday & Saturday for dinner.
Closed Sunday & Monday.
Cash or checks accepted.

A phone call paves the way to Rileybrook Hall where reservations are a must—and be prepared to plan months ahead! Directions are essential and best given by the owner. Prepare yourself for an adventure into rural Franklin County and the country home of Tom and Rob. Meals are served at specific times, and arriving early gives you the opportunity to wander and enjoy the lovely garden. Lunch is always vegetarian, usually pastas with special sauces. The dinner entree is determined by the first person making a reservation for that evening. Choices may be poultry Florentine, roast pork with apples, or beef cordon bleu. Signature items are the potatoes Rileybrook (mashed with carrots, chives, garlic and three cheeses), house salad (red leaf endive tossed with olive oil, garlic, cilantro and lime), and dessert, which is always white chocolate and almond bread pudding with a Jack Daniels sauce. The owners want their guests to feel like they are in someone's home being served by the host, so the number of tables is limited and well worth booking ahead. Rileybrook does not have a liquor license so you may bring a bottle of wine to accompany your meal.

67. CABANA ROOM
30 East Main Street
Brownsburg, IN 46112
(317) 858-8755
Open Monday-Saturday for lunch & dinner. Closed Sunday.
Credit cards accepted.

South of Brownsburg's new town hall is a little restaurant nestled between a jewelry store and a cigar bar. Wooden floors and brick walls that showcase patriotic art give an eclectic look to the restaurant. There's a potpourri of French bread and Caribbean sandwiches for lunch, with the chicken white stromboli and the Cuban the favorites. Everyday, there are six homemade soups. Dinners include chops marinated with Cabana island spices, salmon grilled then baked on a cedar plank, and pasta selections like Tequila fettuccine. Desserts are all made in-house with the carrot cake and Key lime pie being the signature items. You can enjoy a quiet dinner in pleasant surroundings, just a short drive from Indianapolis.

68. CHEZ JEAN
8821 South State Road 67
Camby, IN 46113
(317) 831-0870
Open Tuesday-Saturday for dinner. Closed Sunday & Monday.
Credit cards accepted.

Carl Huckaby, a past American Culinary Federation's National Chef of the Year, creates an intimate and romantic atmosphere for you to enjoy in this wonderful French restaurant. Dining is available in three different settings: the handsome country room, the open and airy garden room, or the more formal French Provincial dining room, each offering authentic French cuisine and a continental special. Dinner includes soup, salad, sorbet, entree, starch, vegetable and ala carte desserts, such as bruleé, souffles, bourbon pecan pie or chocolate mousse. There are 40-50 entrees to choose from with rack of lamb and canard a la orange the house favorites.

69. BUB'S BURGERS & ICE CREAM

210 West Main Street
Carmel, IN 46032
(317) 706-2827
Open daily for lunch & dinner.
Credit cards accepted.

Bub's is a Monon Trail destination, a wonderful reason to take a walk! Yes, Bub is the owner's nickname, but it also stands for "Big Ugly Burger." The "Big Ugly" is a one pound handpattied burger and there's a Wall of Champions with pictures of those who have eaten one. For the less ambitious, there's the half-pound "Not So Ugly" or the quarter-pound "Settle for Less Ugly." The ugly burgers come on custom made rolls and can be accompanied by waffle fries, onion rings or regular fries. There's an elk burger available for low-fat conscious customers. If burgers aren't your thing, there are Black Angus hot dogs, chili, chicken, or Bub's grilled Mahi Mahi sandwiches. Soups are available in bread bowls. Colorful farm scene murals decorate the interior of the ice cream shop in the front of the building. Import/specialty beers and wines are available. Also, look for Bub's Cafe just a short distance away along the Monon Trail, serving breakfast and light lunch.

70. GLASS CHIMNEY BAR

12901 Old Meridian Street
Carmel, IN 46032
(317) 844-0921
Open Monday-Saturday for dinner. Closed Sunday.
Credit cards accepted.

The Glass Chimney is known throughout the state for its delicious continental cuisine. The secret here is the bar area of this fine restaurant. Each month, the bar offers a "special" meal, including a glass of house wine (11 choices) or a draft beer, for under $15.00! Appetizers and desserts from The Glass Chimney menu may also be ordered in the bar. You can be added to the e-mail list and notified of monthly specials. The bar is a cozy place with few tables. Seating is also available on the outdoor deck, where smoking is permitted. No reservations are taken.

71. WOODY'S LIBRARY

40 East Main Street
Carmel, IN 46032
(317) 573-4444
Open daily for lunch & dinner.
Credit cards accepted.

This brick and limestone building was one of 168 libraries built in Indiana in the early 1900's as a gift from steel and railroad tycoon Andrew Carnegie. The interior has been transformed into an upscale restaurant; however, the shelves, books and antiques that are part of the decor preserve the intimate and inviting atmosphere of a small library. The imaginative menu changes daily and is presented to each diner as a page in an actual book. Beef, poultry, veal, pork, and seafood entrees are embellished with wonderful sauces and glazes. Sesame seared tuna steak, tilapia piccata, champagne-citrus chicken, and horseradish-crusted ahi with honey-soy are just a few of the tempting choices! The lunch menu offers several different sandwiches, salads and wraps. Woody's Place is in the basement and is a great spot for more casual dining or to wait for your table upstairs.

72. HERSHBERGER'S ESSENHAUS
223 North Jefferson Street
Converse, IN 46919
(765) 395-5905
Open Monday-Friday for breakfast & lunch; Saturday for lunch;
Thursday & Friday for dinner. Closed Sunday.
Cash or checks accepted.

The red brick building just a few blocks off the main road running through town easily identifies this family-style restaurant. The menu is filled with a wonderful selection of items made from scratch, along with the daily specials offered for breakfast, lunch and dinner. Come with a big appetite on Tuesdays for all-you-can-eat chicken and on Fridays for all-you-can-eat fish! Prime rib is the featured special on Saturdays. Homemade bread and pies are always available with a few more choices added in the summer when fruits are in season. Delicious sugar-free pies are offered for diabetics or calorie watchers!

73. BEEF HOUSE
I-74 & State Road 63
Covington, IN 47932
(765) 793-3947
Open daily for lunch & dinner.
Credit cards accepted.

The Wright family purchased a small restaurant in 1963 and became well-known for their homemade rolls, a recipe secured at Purdue University while majoring in hotel/restaurant management. Today, they continue to be famous for the fact that all of the food served is "homemade," including wonderful soups and delicious pies. If you're in the mood for a terrific steak, this is the place to go!

74. MAPLE CORNER
1126 Liberty Street
Covington, IN 47932
(765) 793-2224
Open Tuesday-Sunday for dinner; Sunday for lunch. Closed Monday.
Credit cards accepted.

This original 1931 roadhouse has been beautifully restored by the present owners and features several different dining rooms, each with its own special atmosphere. Tiffany style windows and lamps add to the homey yet elegant surroundings, as do a variety of antiques and collectibles. Unique to Maple Corner is the use of sassafras and other native Indiana woods over a woodburning fire for grilling choice steaks and fresh seafood. They also feature an award-winning one pound pork chop. The menu reflects the Midwestern tradition of "made from scratch" using locally grown fruits and vegetables. Homemade salad dressings, freshly baked breads and seasonal desserts are a specialty. An in-house bakery also features all homemade items.

75. ARBOR CAFÉ & TEA ROOM

7173 West US 40
Cumberland, IN 46229
(317) 891-1051
Open daily for breakfast & lunch; Thursday-Saturday for dinner.
Credit cards accepted.

Located just east of Indianapolis on US 40 (Washington Street), the owner has reno-vated an old farm house and turned it into a charming café. You can enjoy your meal in one of three warm and inviting dining areas: the Porch, the Green Room, or the more formal Coral Room with its beautiful chandelier. The lunch menu is noted for its wonderful homemade soups, hefty salads and a variety of specialty sandwiches, including the popular BLT. The dinner menu features a nice selection of fresh fish, prime rib, steak and pork, plus meals with an international flair such as the German feast that is available on the first full weekend of every month. The homemade oat-meal cake is a top choice for dessert, along with cheesecake, creme bruleé, and bread pudding with Southern Comfort sauce. With 24 hours' notice and a minimum of four guests, you can arrange for an English Tea or Grand Victorian Tea featuring fruits, finger sandwiches, fresh scones and a variety of cake and pastry creations.

76. MAYBERRY CAFÉ

78 West Main Street
Danville, IN 46122
(317) 745-4067
Open daily for lunch & dinner.
Credit cards accepted.

If you're a fan of the Andy Griffith Show, head to the town square in Danville and look for the squad car parked out front! You will appreciate the many pictures and other memorabilia from the television classic that decorate the interior of this small town restaurant. The café-type decor includes lace tablecloths, brass chandeliers and an Aunt Bee's parlor atmosphere. A little of the big city charm is noticeable in the 40-50 item menu offering ribeye, orange roughy, prime rib, fried chicken and catfish. Make sure you save room for a piece of Aunt Bee's apple pie!

77. STONEHOUSE RESTAURANT & BAKERY

124 East Main Street
Delphi, IN 46923
(765) 564-4663
Open Monday-Saturday for breakfast, lunch & dinner. Closed Sunday.
Credit cards accepted.

This historic building opened as a saloon and brothel in 1874 and continued to house a bar until the 1980's. Today, you'll find a small town, downtown restaurant offering not only breakfast, lunch and dinner, but a bakery filled with homemade breads, pies, cookies and muffins. Breakfast egg dishes are accompanied by a giant cinnamon roll as a side or you might prefer the cinnamon bread French toast. Lunch choices include hamburger, grilled or breaded tenderloin, and various chicken sandwiches, served with chips and pickle. Dinner selections include ham steak with grilled pineapple, rib eye steak, and fried chicken. They invite you to "stop in for real home cookin' today!"

78. WOLFF'S TAVERN
1447 South A Street
Elwood, IN 46036
(765) 552-9022
Open Monday-Saturday for lunch & dinner. Closed Sunday.
Cash or checks accepted.

This small town tavern, located in a century-old building, has tin ceilings from the local tin factory, an old wooden bar, and paintings and beer signs covering the walls. The menu hasn't changed much since the tavern opened, and customers continue to come to Wolff's for the roast beef Manhattans—they make their own gravy!—and breaded tenderloins, plus homemade potato and chili vegetable soups. Other popular items are steaks, cheeseburgers and fish.

79. EUGENE COVERED BRIDGE RESTAURANT
5787 North Main Street
Eugene, IN 47928
(765) 492-7376
Open daily for breakfast, lunch & dinner.
Cash or checks accepted.

Located on the Big Vermillion River, you can look out the back windows of the restaurant and view the second longest single span covered bridge in Indiana. Originally a grocery store and gas station before extensive renovations, it now has the atmosphere of an old country store with framed historical photos covering the walls, mementos of the town history, and license plates from all 50 states plus Canada, Venezuela and Argentina. The menu is simply "good ol' Indiana food" served family style, and catfish is the specialty, along with 28 varieties of homemade pies--coconut cream is a favorite! No alcohol is served.

80. PETERSON'S
7690 East 96th Street
Fishers, IN 46038
(317) 598-8863
Open Monday-Saturday for dinner. Closed Sunday.
Credit cards accepted.

Peterson's boasts "Only the Very Best" and clearly lives up to its commitment. Locally owned by Joe Peterson and chef Karl Benko, the restaurant provides one-of-a-kind steak and seafood entrees in the spirit of regional American cuisine. Maine lobster, Maine diver sea scallops in a pinot and mushroom risotto, and Atlantic swordfish "mignon" are outstanding choices. Prime grade steaks and chops are attractively presented on a plate with colorful vegetables. Peterson's has been recognized with an Award of Excellence from the Wine Spectator and also has a nice selection of premium vodkas, malt scotches and barrel bourbons. The full dinner menu is available in the lounge where live music is featured on weekends.

81. AUNTIE M'S TEAROOM & DESSERTS
154 East Jefferson
Franklin, IN 46131
(317) 346-4007
Open Tuesday-Saturday for lunch & tea. Closed Sunday & Monday.
Credit cards accepted.

Auntie M's honors the 1700 British tradition of taking an afternoon break, enjoying conversation and a good cup of tea. There are wonderful desserts to go with the tea, and the menu suggests, "Yes, you can have dessert first!" Homemade soups, salads and sandwiches are served with sweet potato chips, a unique treat. High tea, so named because it was usually enjoyed sitting atop stools or standing up in a tea shop, is recommended and includes assorted sandwiches and scones with Morganshire cream. Doilies, teapots of all shapes and sizes, an antique curio cabinet, and pictures of English royals decorate the restaurant.

82. RICHARD'S KITCHEN
229 South Main Street
Franklin, IN 46131
(317) 738-5451
Open Tuesday-Friday for lunch & dinner;
Saturday for dinner. Closed Sunday & Monday.
Credit cards accepted.

Richard has settled in Franklin after successful culinary experiences in Aspen, Knoxville and Philadelphia. His wife is from Franklin so it was a logical place for him to open his own restaurant. One block south of the Johnson County Courthouse, you could expect to slip in for a quick, ordinary meal. However, there is nothing ordinary about the menu! The specialty is prime rib, but you will also find creatively prepared options such as chicken in a mushroom-marsala wine sauce, pork tenderloin in a spicy-sweet sauce, or grilled wild salmon with tropical fruit salsa. For lunch, there's chili made with prime rib, salmon cakes, Angus burgers, and portabello mushroom sandwiches along with a variety of salads. For dessert, you might try the molten chocolate cake. The open kitchen has six seats nearby where you can watch everything being made from scratch. A carefully selected range of wine and spirits is available. Richard's Kitchen presents casual dining with a flair in a non-smoking environment. Outdoor seating is available in the summer.

83. THE WILLARD
99 North Main Street
Franklin, IN 46131
(317) 738-9668
Open daily for lunch & dinner.
Credit cards accepted.

The original brick home built on this site in 1860 is the core of the present structure. Eliza Willard and her niece and nephew, the Judahs, constructed a hotel around the home in 1922. Interestingly, Mrs. Willard and Mrs. Judah were active in the Prohibition Movement and today the space is occupied by a pub and eatery! When the property was refurbished, care was taken to maintain the antique fixtures, the curved wooden staircase and the marble fireplace. The specialty is pizza, made by hand, but there is an extensive list of appetizer, sandwich and salad choices for family dining. Mexican dishes, steak, chicken and seafood entrees are also on the menu. The Willard is touted as a place "where friends meet" for a drink and a bite to eat, and the outdoor seating area is a popular place to gather in nice weather.

84. ALMOST HOME

17 West Franklin Street
Greencastle, IN 46135
(765) 653-5788
Open Monday-Saturday for lunch & dinner; Sunday for brunch.
Credit cards accepted.

Window boxes filled with wildflowers decorate the entrance to this charming restaurant and gift shop, specializing in delicious homemade soups, croissant sandwiches, salads and delectable desserts, plus a dinner menu that changes each evening. Beer and wine are also available. The "homey" interior is a comfortable spot for friends to meet for a relaxing meal. You will enjoy browsing in the gift shop featuring a unique collection of antique and vintage furniture, a vast selection of gifts for any occasion, home decor items, and collectibles. Surrounded by friendly people in a bright and cheerful setting, you feel as if you're "almost home!"

85. BREAD LADIES

5 American Legion Place
Greenfield, IN 46140
(317) 462-3315
Open Monday-Friday for continental breakfast & lunch;
Friday night for dinner. Closed Saturday & Sunday.
Credit cards accepted.

As you walk into this storefront bakery and café, you see the bread ladies at work in the kitchen. Checkered tablecloths add a welcoming look to the dining room with local paintings covering the brick walls. Using only natural ingredients and no additives, the Bread Ladies have been hand-making breads for over 10 years and have developed a "style" all their own. Daily bread selections include the popular herb peasant, honey maple oatmeal, wheat, white and 8-grain. There are also freshly baked muffins and chocolate brownies that make your mouth water when you think about them days later! The signature salad is a chicken salad topped with sugared almonds and sweet vinaigrette dressing. In addition, there is a nice assortment of tasty sandwiches, wraps and gourmet soups on the menu. Italian sodas and espressos are also available.

86. CARNEGIE'S
100 West North Street
Greenfield, IN 46140
(317) 462-8480

Open Tuesday-Saturday for dinner. Closed Sunday & Monday.
Credit cards accepted.

The downstairs area of the former Carnegie library provides a unique, inviting and cozy setting for diners to enjoy their meal. Dark green walls create the perfect backdrop for the artwork displayed throughout the restaurant. While dining at Carnegie's, you must take a tour of the herb gardens and see the outdoor Roman style wood-fired oven used for baking breads. The chef, trained in Florence, Italy, offers a menu that changes with the seasons and focuses on gourmet dishes presented as an art form. Creative dinner entrees feature ossobuco (veal shank), duck breast, salmon and pork tenderloin. Carnegie's offers catering, and the upper floor is available for parties.

87. BAY WINDOW
3115-A Meridian Park Drive
Greenwood, In 46142
(317) 882-1330
Open Monday-Saturday for breakfast & lunch; Sunday for breakfast.
Dinners to go Monday-Thursday.
Cash or checks accepted.

There isn't actually a bay window, but there are doilies, glass cups, flowered tablecloths, garden paintings and a wonderful selection of breakfast and luncheon fare. Weekly specials feature a type of sandwich, quiche, soup or croissant plus regular sandwich choices of egg, tuna or chicken salad, turkey, corned beef, and ham. There are also four different homemade soups offered daily, with two of the choices always being cream of broccoli and cheddar cheese. Save room for the homemade desserts: French Silk Pie, Raspberry Royale, Oowie Goowie Cake with rum sauce, and a Liberace Sundae, to name just a few!

88. CASA MIGUEL'S
102 South Madison
Greenwood, IN 46142
(317) 888-9010
Open Monday-Saturday for lunch & dinner. Closed Sunday.
Cash, checks or debit cards accepted.

In 1988, a desire to go into the restaurant business, combined with an appreciation for Mexican food acquired through many trips to Mexico, led the owners to open Casa Miguel's. The original cook, whose roots were in Mexico, had a talent for preparing tasty, authentic dishes made from scratch, using fresh ingredients and no preservatives. The chili con queso and "chimi-chihuahuas" (miniature chimi-changas) are his special creations. Flautas, served with a pleasingly spicy sauce, are popular for lunch. The dinner menu offers everything from tacos to fajitas, the house specialty prepared with a choice of pork, steak or marinated chicken. For the less adventurous diner, the menu also includes many American food options. Dessert features their famous hojulas (sugar cookies) served with coffee.

89. WELLIVER'S

On State Road 38
Hagerstown, IN 47346
(765) 489-4131
Open Thursday-Saturday for dinner; Sunday for lunch & dinner.
Credit cards accepted.

In 1947, Guy Welliver bought a restaurant in Hagerstown that seated 50 people. Today, there is a seating capacity of 500! The buffet features over 100 items, including the steamed shrimp and pan-fried chicken that has made them famous throughout the area, and you'll love the fresh baked cinnamon bread. Snow crab legs are available on Fridays. You may also choose to order from the menu, and some recommend that you select one of the booths in the bar.

90. AGIO

635 Massachusetts Avenue
Indianapolis, IN 46204
(317) 488-0359
Open Tuesday-Friday for lunch & dinner; Saturday & Sunday for dinner.
Closed Monday.
Credit cards accepted.

Located in the Massachusetts Avenue Arts District close to historic Lockerbie Square, this Italian/Mediterranean restaurant is known for its innovative cuisine, gracious service, and unique decor. A sign "Mettiti a tuo agio," meaning "make yourself at home," greets you at the entrance. The owner has created a stylish upscale atmosphere for dining at affordable prices, making it a popular choice for visitors. The menu changes seasonally and features tempting entrees such as grilled lamb, veal scallopini, pork tenderloin stuffed with prosciutto, and a variety of pasta dishes. The dinner salad with field greens, pistachio, and green olives is exceptionally light and tasty. After dining, enjoy a stroll through the historic neighborhood. Reservations are recommended on weekends.

91. AMALFI RISTORANTE ITALIANO

1351 West 86th Street
Indianapolis, IN 46260
(317) 253-4034
Open Monday-Friday for lunch & dinner; Saturday for dinner. Closed Sunday.
Credit cards accepted.

Why the name "Amalfi?" Is it named after the spectacular blue coastal waters of Southern Italy?..or ladies' shoes? Regardless, the name was suggested by many of our "Dining Secrets" readers as a restaurant that "must" be included in the guide. Family owned and operated, you can enjoy authentic Italian cuisine in an intimate, fine dining setting with beautiful Italian landscape paintings. Chef's specialty dishes include eggplant parmesan, tortellini Michelangelo, spaghetti carbonara, filet mignon and various seafood, veal and chicken dishes which are certain to satisfy any pallet. Don't forget to try the homemade tiramisu and lemoncello. For "A Taste of Italy That's Around the Corner, Not Around the World[SM]," visit Amalfi. Reservations are recommended. All guests must be 21 years of age or older.

92. ATHENS ON 86TH STREET
2284 West 86th Street
Indianapolis, IN 46260
(317) 879-8644
Open Tuesday-Sunday for lunch & dinner. Closed Monday.
Credit cards accepted.

A friendly atmosphere greets you as you enter this Greek restaurant. The Norwegian/ Greek owners have used structural columns and lots of open space to create an environment that feels like an upscale European cafe. There is also outdoor seating, weather permitting, and a banquet room for large groups. The table staff takes pleasure in explaining and helping you choose your meal. The familiar Greek specialties like spanikopita, gyros, mousaka, dolmathes and kabobs are available, but you owe yourself the pleasure of trying something new, such as yemista, lahanodolmathes, or gigantes. Of course, there is fileto, pork chops and lamb chops for the less adventurous diner! Off-site catering is available.

93. BAZBEAUX PIZZA
334 Massachusetts Avenue
Indianapolis, IN 46204
(317) 636-7662
Open daily for lunch & dinner.
Credit cards accepted.

Bazbeaux was the whimsical name given to a court jester, whose cleverness was used to create new dishes to amuse the courts he served. In 1986, the Bazbeaux legend was brought to Indianapolis as the first restaurant in the area to introduce pizza lovers to a new concept: unique combinations of sometimes exotic toppings on a choice of wheat or white crust. Building on the success of the Broad Ripple location, they expanded to this old store building in "downtown's art and theater district." Lunch specials include pizza by the slice. Pizza alla quattro formaggio is the most popular--five cheeses, bacon and mushrooms. The muffaletta and stromboli sandwiches are also in demand. Desserts have been added to the menu--try the popular tartufo or sorbetti. A nice selection of beers and wines is available. While you're there, look at the beautiful designs by local artists decorating the interior.

94. BOSPHORUS ISTANBUL CAFE
935 South East Street
Indianapolis, IN 46225
(317) 974-1770
Open daily for lunch & dinner.
Credit cards accepted.

The little clapboard house at this address has a sign that identifies it as Bosphorus Cafe; otherwise, it might not be clear that you have found Indianapolis' first Turkish restaurant. As you step inside, however, the music, the painted floors, the pictures, the people and the menu assure you that you are at the right place. Turkish names are given to the various food items, but good English explanations are printed on the menu. Appetizers include hummus, eggplant salsa and falafel. Kebabs, stuffed eggplant, and gyros are familiar choices but if you're feeling adventurous, try Ispanklitavuk (spinach chicken) or Iskender (slices of doner on grilled bread cubes with tomato sauce). Seafood specialties and veggie dishes are also available, and you might want to try the Ayran, an interesting Turkish yogurt drink.

95. BOULEVARD PLACE CAFE
4155 North Boulevard
Indianapolis, IN 46208
(317) 283-2233
Open Monday for lunch; Tuesday-Friday for lunch & dinner;
Saturday & Sunday for brunch.
Credit cards accepted.

A delightful respite off the beaten track is located on this Boulevard Place corner. Your eyes will immediately be attracted to the colorful artwork on the walls as you settle into the casual ambiance of this neighborhood cafe. Choose from a variety of sandwiches and salads and make sure someone in your group orders the homemade potato chips. Also, check out the board each day for the daily specials—they are not to be ignored! On Saturday and Sunday, stop after church or exercise for breakfast casseroles, hash, omelettes, pancakes, French toast, and other tasty combinations.

96. BROAD RIPPLE STEAK HOUSE
929 East Westfield Boulevard
Indianapolis, IN 46220
(317) 253-8101
Open Monday-Saturday for dinner. Closed Sunday.
Credit cards accepted.

Filled with shops, art galleries, bars and restaurants, Broad Ripple Village is a fun and lively area where you can enjoy that small town feeling as you stroll the streets and choose a place to eat. The Broad Ripple Steak House is in a lovely white house on a corner south of the canal, right across from the Monon Trail. A table by a window is a great place to sit so you can watch the sidewalk traffic while enjoying your meal. Rich colors, contemporary art and subdued lighting provide an upscale dining venue where the menu has a lot more to offer than just steak! For instance, jambalaya, olive oil poached tilapia, honey mustard crusted lamb rack, and mushroom and herb strudel are other temptations. Chef Features change weekly and the bleu cheese crusted filet is one of the favorites. Live entertainment can be enjoyed Thursday through Saturday.

97. CAPRI RISTORANTE ITALIANO

2602 Ruth Drive (74th & North Keystone)
Indianapolis, IN 46240
(317) 259-4122
Open daily for lunch & dinner.
Credit cards accepted.

Arturo, your host, has created a sophisticated, attractive environment from what used to be a neighborhood hangout. Fresh flowers, high ceilings, outside dining and a fireside venue in the bar make for an upscale destination restaurant. His creations are prepared from family recipes, and there is often a family member in the kitchen. Daily specials, like squash filled raviolis, always show imagination and are outstanding. Grilled eggplant, mozzarella prosciutto or gamberoni (shrimp) in white wine are excellent antipasti. The pasta dishes, such as ravioli aurora (ricotta & spinach filling) and pennetta bosciaola (portabella mushrooms with penne pasta), are hard to pass up. For the main course, there's always a fresh fish of the day, but you may want veal, chicken or a filet instead. All of the meals are served by a gracious staff under the experienced supervision of your host.

98. DUFOUR'S IN IRVINGTON

5648 East Washington Street
Indianapolis, IN 46219
(317) 357-1696
Open Tuesday-Saturday for breakfast & lunch. Closed Sunday & Monday.
Credit cards accepted.

Indianapolis has some wonderful historic neighborhoods and Irvington is one of them. Bernadette, the owner, grew up practically next door to her restaurant. In fact, she took pleasure in knowing that her mother was watching out the window of her nearby home as Bernadette converted an old hardware store into the neighborhood eatery it is today. Each day there is a special feature and fresh bread. The daily menu might include creamed chip beef, a pasta platter, corned beef on rye, beef and noodles, or another creative recipe. For breakfast, you might try the country skillet omelet. Dufour's is a good place to stop when you visit the antique stores in the area. It is a smoke-free environment.

99. DUNAWAY'S

351 South East Street
Indianapolis, IN 46204
(317) 638-7663
Open Monday-Friday for lunch & dinner;
Saturday & Sunday for dinner.
Credit cards accepted.

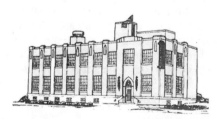

In order to preserve an architectural treasure, Historic Landmarks Foundation of Indiana moved the 735 ton Indiana Oxygen Building to its current location in 1995. Yes, this 1930 structure was, at the time of its move, the heaviest building ever moved in the USA! Jeff Dunaway saw the possibilities of applying his St. Elmo's restaurant experience to a unique, historic environment, so he bought the property.

He worked hard to preserve its historic features while inventively introducing an art deco style with industrial motifs. The building is not the only story about Dunaway's! For lunch, there are sandwiches (focaccia BLT, burgers, grilled portabello wrap), salads (lobster and avocado, warm mushroom) and entrees of porcini mushroom stuffed ravioli, seared sea scallops, grilled chicken pesto, or the daily red plate specials. Dinner might begin with a Dunaway's shrimp cocktail with "fire and brimstone" horseradish sauce, seared yellowfin tuna, or calamari fritte appetizers. Then, choose an entree from the chops menu (Colorado lamb chops, NY strip steak, filet mignon) or one of the specialties (lobster ravioli, grilled quail, veal, grilled hanger steak). There are many tasty, well-prepared items. Dunaway's also has open-air rooftop dining available, weather permitting.

100. ELEMENTS
415 North Alabama Street
Indianapolis, IN 46204
(317) 634-8888
Open Tuesday-Saturday for dinner.
Closed Sunday & Monday.
Credit cards accepted.

＝L＝M＝NT5

Described by several people as Indy's "best," Elements is located on Alabama Street at the spot where Massachusetts Avenue begins to angle. The restaurant overlooks a little urban garden where dining outside is encouraged in warm weather. The cuisine is described as contemporary American, which means a good mix of French, Asian and Mediterranean--a wonderful combination of flavors. The menu changes daily, and could include the Kurobuta pork chop with cumin-studded polenta, or grilled quail with spinach and ricotta salata cheese. Of course, there are also soups, salads and appetizers on the menu that make your mouth water just reading about them! Dining at Elements is a truly special treat.

101. EL MOROCCO
1260 West 86th Street
Indianapolis, IN 46260
(317) 844-1104
Open Tuesday-Sunday for dinner. Closed Monday.
Credit cards accepted.

You'll enter this restaurant through a beaded curtain and immediately notice the dim lights, the tapestries on the walls, and many tables low to the ground with pillows for seats. You're in Morocco in Indianapolis! Warm cloths are brought to cleanse your hands before eating. It might be a buffet night, but ordering from the menu is always possible. The host describes the specials for the evening and graciously answers any menu questions. A suggested dinner could include five courses: first course, Harriara Soup (tomato, lentil, chickpeas and celery); second course, Bakoula (spinach appetizer) and Msharmal (carrot with paprika, lemon juice and cilantro); third course, Bastela (filo pastry with chicken, egg and almond); fourth course, the entree, perhaps a Kabab or Couscous Bidaoui; and fifth course, dessert—usually seasonal fruits and baklava. Belly dancers entertain on Friday and Saturday nights.

102. G.T. SOUTH'S RIB HOUSE

5711 East 71st Street
Indianapolis, IN 46220
(317) 849-6997
Open Monday-Saturday for lunch & dinner. Closed Sunday.
Credit cards accepted.

As you enter G.T. South's Rib House, the aroma of smoked BBQ fills the air and whets the appetite. The founder hailed from the south and wanted to bring authentic barbecue to Indianapolis. He claimed that barbecue chefs argue about whose barbecue is the best, but they all agree: "Cook it low and smoke it slow." The pulled pork sandwich with hot or mild sauce, served with your choice of a side dish and chips, is clearly the most popular item, but smoked turkey and beef brisket are also available. For larger appetites, the baby back ribs (served "wet" or "dry") and rib tips dinners are truly satisfying. A full-service bar with big screen television and a player piano provides entertainment in a very casual and relaxed setting.

103. H₂0 SUSHI

1912 Broad Ripple Avenue
Indianapolis, IN 46220
(317) 254-0677
Open Tuesday-Saturday for dinner. Closed Sunday & Monday.
Credit cards accepted.

Sushi bars are fun places to gather for conversation, libation and sushi treats! H_2O invites you to stop in, relax, ask questions and enjoy. What is the difference between Nigiri and Sashimi? Nigiri has filets of fish on pads of rice, Sashimi is just the fish filets! You might want to begin with an appetizer of Edamame or be more adventurous with tuna tartar. There are salads and soups to choose from as well, but the best part is the "rolls." Besides the familiar California rolls, there's a Joe Pesci, T-N-T, salmon cigar, spicy octopus, and a variety of others. The sake bomb is an added treat!

104. HARRY & IZZY'S

153 South Illinois Street
Indianapolis, IN 46225
(317) 635-9594
Open daily for lunch & dinner.
Credit cards accepted.

Looking at the logo, old time customers will recognize the silhouettes of Harry and Izzy, owners of St. Elmo's from 1947-1986. The choice of name is a tribute to the men and also establishes a sister connection to the restaurant right down the street. While sharing a few classic dishes from the St. Elmo's menu, Harry & Izzy's offers more variety. There are ten different appetizers in addition to the famous St. Elmo starter shrimp cocktail. Of course, steaks are on the menu but there are other choices: seafood, chops, chicken, pasta, sandwiches and brick oven baked pizza. Sides are available, including the traditional house-cut fries. The ambiance is sophisticated with comfortable seating in four different rooms plus open seating at the bar.

105. HOAGLIN TO GO CAFE & MARKETPLACE

448 Massachusetts Avenue
Indianapolis, IN 46204
(317) 423-0300
Open daily for breakfast & lunch. Market open in evenings.
Credit cards accepted.

Hoaglin To Go is a great early morning stop after a hike or church, or just to hang out and read your newspaper. Breakfasts include omelettes, quiche, and oatmeal with the weekends offering additional items like French toast, Scotch eggs, eggs Benedict and coffee any way you want. For lunch, you can order a sandwich or salad from the menu or choose from the daily specials featuring quiche, soup and more. The housemade foccacia bread is a great addition to any sandwich. Breakfast and lunch can be eaten in this contemporary cafe or their unique meals can be carried out. The marketplace is open after 2:30 pm so you can stop for a tasty dinner to take home.

106. HOLLYHOCK HILL

8110 North College Avenue
Indianapolis, IN 46240
(317) 251-2294
Open Tuesday-Saturday for dinner; Sunday for
lunch & dinner. Closed Monday.
Credit cards accepted.

In 1928, the original owners began serving dinners at their Country Cottage in northern Marion County. Because of the many beautiful hollyhocks on the premises, it soon became known as Hollyhock Hill. One of a few family-style restaurants still in existence in the U.S., Hollyhock stands out from others not only for the excellent food but for its more formal ambience created by floral curtains and fresh flowers on the tables in each of the light and airy dining rooms. Steaks and shrimp are on the menu, but the fried chicken "like mother used to make" is the most popular, accompanied by a feast of vegetables, salad with their famous sweet-sour dressing, homemade pickled beets, apple butter and homemade biscuits. Ice cream with a choice of toppings to make your own sundae completes this memorable dining experience.

107. IARIA'S ITALIAN RESTAURANT

317 South College Avenue
Indianapolis, IN 46202
(317) 638-7706
Open Tuesday-Friday for lunch & dinner; Saturday for dinner.
Closed Sunday & Monday.
Credit cards accepted.

The Iaria family came to the United States from Calabria, located at the very tip of the boot of Italy. This family-owned restaurant opened in 1932 and continues to offer wonderful Italian dishes prepared from recipes passed down through generations. Very little of the original decor has changed over the years, but the comfortable atmosphere makes it an inviting place to bring the family. The lunch and dinner menus are the same, offering meat and spinach ravioli, meatballs and Italian sausage, pizza, pastas served with your choice of sauces, plus delicious homemade garlic bread. There are weekly specials as well. You'll also enjoy the cheesecake, cannoli, or spumoni for dessert.

108. ICE HOUSE
2352 South West Street
Indianapolis, IN 46225
(317) 788-7075
Open Monday-Saturday for lunch & dinner. Closed Sunday.
Credit cards accepted.

Calling itself "Indy's Coolest Lunch Spot," the Ice House definitely draws downtown workers to its ice house door. The building really looks pretty new, but much of the memorabilia and furnishings inside this bar are from old downtown structures. Neon signs capture the eye: HONEST, Merricks Real Estate, Dry Cleaning & Laundry. A commanding portrait of a suit-clad gentleman of the 1930's looks down on the bar's patrons. The fun is that no one knows who he is! Sandwiches come in baskets with the half-pound burgers and giant breaded tenderloins the favorites. A variety of steaks plus chicken and catfish are listed as entrees for dinner. Appetizers are plentiful, and there's always free popcorn.

109. ICHIBAN NOODLES SUSHI RESTAURANT
8355 Bash Street
Indianapolis, IN 46250
(317) 841-0484
Open Monday-Saturday for lunch & dinner. Closed Sunday.
Credit cards accepted.

On the road to the Castleton Post Office, there's a little white house with a handmade sign that says "noodles." Don't be fooled by the outside! The colorful interior of this small, well-organized restaurant is filled with stained glass, origami bird mobiles, paper lantern-like lights, and booths and tables tucked into nooks and crannies. The sushi bar is set up at the entrance and Louis, the owner, prepares the rolls and the nigiri (rice with fish on top). Bento crates (boxes with compartments for different food items) are a good choice for variety. Donburi (bowl with stew over rice) is on the menu as are three types of noodles (ramen, udon, soba) served different ways. Classic entrees of chicken, pork, seafood and steak will more than satisfy those not interested in sushi. Japanese beer and sake are available.

110. JASMINE THAI RESTAURANT
4825 East 96th Street
Indianapolis, IN 46240
(317) 848-8950
Open Monday-Friday for lunch & dinner; Saturday & Sunday for dinner.
Credit cards accepted.

Jasmine's provides you with a wonderful opportunity to eat a healthy meal! The restaurant offers soups, salads, rice and noodle dishes, Thai curries and some traditional meals. Lunch specials are offered during the week. The satay and salad rolls are tasty appetizers. Drunken noodles (pad ki-mao) and Panang curry are flavor-filled entrees. The staff, many of whom are related to the owner, takes pride in pleasing the customers. If you have any concerns about mild, medium or hot, the servers understand and accommodate, even if the meal needs to be sent back to the kitchen! Vegetarian requests are honored, too.

111. JUDGE'S BBQ

2104 West Michigan Street
Indianapolis, IN 46222
(317) 631-0340
Open Monday-Friday 11am-6pm. Closed Saturday & Sunday.
Credit cards accepted.

Walk in the door, place your order, listen for the bell, look for your number on the electronic board, and then enjoy Judge's BBQ! There's pork ribs and chicken, rib tips, pulled pork and other varieties of sandwiches, wings, and smoked salmon. Sweet potatoes and other items are available on the side, along with the highly recommended corn casserole. This family-owned restaurant is housed in a renovated space across the street from the Haughville Library and features richly colored and polished wooden tables of all heights and sizes. It's a great place to have a lunch meeting where you can spread out your work on the large square tables. The history of the neighborhood and its landmarks is presented through pictures on the walls.

112. MAMA CAROLLA'S

1031 East 54th Street
Indianapolis, IN 46220
(317) 259-9412
Open Tuesday-Saturday for dinner. Closed Sunday & Monday.
Credit cards accepted.

With a desire to authenticate the look of the Italian "mom and pop" restaurants of Omaha, Nebraska, the owners of Mama Carolla's found what they were looking for in this 1920's California stucco, Mediterranean-style home. Wrought iron and white brick create the feeling of dining in a café, terrace restaurant or a lovely home in Spain or Italy. Entrees offer a choice of steak, veal, chicken, salmon, tuna or uniquely tasty pasta dishes. Specialties include pasta carbonara, chicken rigatoni, rosemary chicken lasagna and Uncle Dino's or Cousin Mary's steak. For dessert lovers, there's tiramisu, cannoli, or a dish of spumoni.

113. OAKLEYS BISTRO

1464 West 86th Street
Indianapolis, IN 46260
(317) 824-1231
Open Tuesday-Saturday for lunch & dinner. Closed Sunday & Monday.
Credit cards accepted.

The food here reflects the creative experience that chef-proprietor Steve Oakley gained while working at famous restaurants such as Lutece in New York City and Charlie Trotter's in Chicago. The menu is designed to be "seasonal and innovative," so it changes monthly. The presentation is like a picture, inviting you to taste and enjoy. Possible lunch items might include soup and your choice of lobster, chicken or salmon tart, duck pizza, shrimp risotto, or meatloaf with barbecue glaze. Along with a tempting selection of dinner appetizers, typical entrees might feature char-broiled lamb loin, poached salmon, and duck breast with wild mushrooms. Indulge in a dessert after your meal: chocolate raspberry torte and rum pound cake are two of the possible choices. Oakleys is a culinary pleasure enjoyed in comfortable surroundings.

114. OH YUMM! BISTRO

5615 North Illinois Street
Indianapolis, IN 46208
(317) 251-5656
Open Monday-Saturday for lunch & dinner. Closed Sunday.
Credit cards accepted.

As a caterer, the owner was frequently asked what she was cooking when preparing food for an event. When she mentioned the menu items, people would typically respond, "Oh, yumm!" So, when she had the opportunity to fulfill her dream of opening a restaurant, Oh Yumm was a natural choice. While shopping at 56th and Illinois, you can take a break and enjoy the seasonal menu offerings which are described as "infusing American and international cuisine with a hint of contemporary comfort food." Lunch might include an hors d'oeuvre of Moroccan shrimp, a steak and potato salad, pescato tacos, or the bistro burger. For a dinner hors d'oeuvre, try the ahi tuna. The house salad, filled with gorgonzola cheese, toasted pine nuts and dried cherries, is a good choice before a main course of hoisin marinated pork loin or bowtie shrimp scampi. Dine inside or outside in nice weather and enjoy the creative flair of Oh Yumm's menu.

115. R bistro

888 Massachusetts Avenue
Indianapolis, IN 46204
(317) 423-0312
Open Monday-Friday for lunch; Wednesday-Saturday for dinner.
Closed Sunday.
Credit cards accepted.

Located in the Massachusetts Avenue Arts District, R bistro offers the kind of eclectic fare expected from a restaurant found on a strip known for its art galleries. The menu, which changes weekly, features internationally influenced contemporary American food that utilizes the freshest ingredients, many of which come from right here in Indiana. Its changing nature makes R bistro one of the most unique dining experiences in the city, and keeps it as unexpected and new as the art found on its neighbor's walls. Though small by comparison (5 appetizers, 5 entrees, 5 desserts), the menu covers a lot of ground by offering at least one meat, one poultry, one fish, one vegetarian and one "comfort food" item each week, providing an infinite number of possibilities for your enjoyment.

116. RALPH'S GREAT DIVIDE

743 East New York Street
Indianapolis, IN 46202
(317) 637-2192
Open Monday-Friday for lunch & dinner.
Closed Saturday & Sunday.
Credit cards accepted.

As you walk through the door, your attention is immediately drawn to the walls filled with Indiana history. Sketches, sports memorabilia, restaurant critic comments, tributes to family member Ralph, and a license plate that belonged to a former governor are just a few examples. Behind the bar there is an old walk-in cooler dating back to the 1930's filled with beer, and there are cases of beer stacked against the wall! Beginning with the listing of "unusual hours," the menu is fun to read. Ralph's is known for its "Hot Pot Aug,"" a cream of potato soup au gratin. There's also a "Hot Pot Pig" which adds bacon and hot pepper cheese. Crackers, melon and a piece of candy are served with the soup. There is quite a variety of sandwiches to choose from, some with catchy names like "The Ethel," "The Lucy" and the horsey mushroom burger, and the club sandwiches are "recommended by local law enforcement agencies." A trip to Ralph's is a delightful experience!

117. RATHSKELLER RESTAURANT
401 East Michigan Street
Indianapolis, IN 46204
(317) 636-0396
Open daily for lunch & dinner.
Credit cards accepted.

Social organizations were an important tradition for early German immigrants in Indianapolis. Thus, in 1894, plans were initiated to build a large club house as a social, cultural, recreational and sports center. An interesting trivia fact—the Normal college courses in physical education that were taught in this building helped establish physical education in schools. Through this connection, IUPUI is considered to be the oldest school of physical education in the country. Today, this elaborately ornate building with its brick facade, slate roof, leaded glass windows and gables is home to many entertainment and dining events. The Rathskeller feels like an old German beer cellar: the sites, the smells, the food, the beer. Deutsche schnitzel, rouladen, sauerbraten, wurst, red cabbage and spaetzle are available, but the menu offers many other choices as well: seafood, pasta, steak and even some vegetarian. Visiting the Rathskeller is both a culinary and historical treat!

118. RESTAURANT AT THE VILLA
1456 North Delaware Street
Indianapolis, IN 46202
(317) 916-8500
Open Monday-Saturday for dinner. Closed Sunday.
Credit cards accepted.

Mother and daughter have teamed up to present the public with the experience of dining in one of Indianapolis' charming old homes. Guests wait in the high-ceiling foyer with a staircase that leads to the dining room. The entry to the Florentine-designed dining room is eye-catching with its commanding windows and artwork adorning the walls. Wherever seated, the food is the focus with a menu that offers innovative, heart healthy choices using the freshest local produce and leanest cuts of meat. The cuisine is prepared without butter or heavy cream, providing guests with a deceptively nutritious dining experience. Guest rooms and a spa are also available at the Villa Inn.

119. ROCK-COLA 50'S CAFE

5730 Brookville Road
Indianapolis, IN 46219
(317) 357-2233
Open Tuesday-Saturday for breakfast & lunch. Closed Sunday & Monday.
Cash only establishment.

This 50's diner in the midst of Indianapolis factories is a great neighborhood gathering place. You can eat at the counter on a revolving stool or in one of the booths; either place, you will be kept busy looking at all the 50's memorabilia on the walls and ceiling while waiting for your order. You can also watch your food being prepared on the open grill. All of the meats are handcut and the grilled tenderloin starts about two inches thick. The cook takes a cleaver, has everyone step back, and then pounds it flat right on the grill! The sandwiches are served on fresh bakery buns with a knife sticking straight up, inviting you to cut into them. Hamburgers, veggie burgers, B-L-T and a Poor Boy's Delite are popular choices, but the Philly is reported to be the best. Of course, there are milkshakes; malts; and vanilla, chocolate and lemon cokes. In addition to some of the meats mentioned, special breakfast entrees ("City Slicker," "Trailer Park" and "Lumberjack") combine eggs with pork chops, ham steak and bacon. On Saturday, there's a breakfast buffet that offers it all!

120. RUTH'S KEYSTONE CAFE

3443 East 86th Street
Indianapolis, IN 46240
(317) 466-0770
Open Monday-Friday for breakfast & lunch; Saturday & Sunday for brunch.
Credit cards accepted

Ruth's Café is the owner's tribute to the memory of his mother and her reputation for gracious hospitality. Family, friends, acquaintances, and anyone who needed a sanctuary were always invited into Ruth's kitchen where homemade dinners and Norwegian delicacies were a staple at her kitchen table. You'll find the same commitment to hospitality at this warm and inviting cafe where you can enjoy a change from the usual breakfast and lunchtime fare. Unique omelets, benedicts and quiches are filled with fresh and flavorful ingredients, such as the smoked salmon or spinach omelet and Eggs a la Crossing, a combination of poached eggs, asparagus and apple smoked bacon, topped with hollandaise sauce. Wonderful homemade soups, salads and tasty sandwiches are available for lunch, and the spinach melt is reported to be "excellent!" Homemade Lefse, a traditional Norwegian potato flat bread with butter and sugar, is also served in Ruth's honor.

121. SAKURA RESTAURANT

7201 North Keystone Avenue
Indianapolis, IN 46240
(317) 259-4171
Open Monday-Saturday for lunch & dinner; Sunday for dinner.
Credit cards accepted.

The parking lot around this white house on North Keystone is always full at lunch or dinner time—a sign of good food! At the same location for almost ten years, Sakura introduced many Indianapolis residents to the sushi concept. The restaurant is filled with pictures of people who have eaten here, letting you know you are in good company! You can sit and watch the sushi being made or take a booth. For lunch, a box is a unique selection with different combinations of rolls, tempura, sushi and sashimi. Sushi can be ordered ala carte as nigiri (fish topped rice), rolls or a combination. Soba (gray buckwheat pasta) or udon (thick white soft wheat) noodles and donburi (rice bowls) are available, as well as a number of Japanese dinners. Your server can help you with your selection. Try it—it's healthy and you'll like it.

122. SANTORINI GREEK KITCHEN
1417 East Prospect Street
Indianapolis, IN 46203
(317) 917-1117
Open Monday-Saturday for lunch & dinner. Closed Sunday.
Credit cards accepted.

Santorini's is located just a few blocks east of the fountain in historic Fountain Square. You can experience the flavors of Greece as you sit in a crisp blue and white-walled restaurant with white linen tablecloths and a very family friendly atmosphere. Food portions are extremely generous and the choices are too! A combination of appetizers or platters is the best way to experience the variety of offerings. Saganaki (their famous "flaming cheese") is a treat to your eyes as well as your taste buds! Other specialties include tomato balls, Taki's famous potatoes, and "Lamb Lovers." For the main course, a nice selection of sandwiches and platters is available: gyros, falafel, dolmades, tiropita, spanokopita, souvlaki, plus many more! Greek wines and beers are on hand to complement your meal. Banquet and meeting facilities are available.

123. SAWASDEE
1222 West 86th Street
Indianapolis, IN 46260
(317) 844-9451
Open Monday-Saturday for lunch & dinner.
Dinner on Sunday.
Credit cards accepted.

Thai food has become very popular and Mr. Ty's family has been educating the Sawasdee patrons for several years. The menu has pictures and good descriptions, but there is always someone available to help the inexperienced figure out what to order and how spicy to make the dish. Soup and a spring roll or Thai salad are served with all of the entrees. The curry dishes are very special but you may select the old standby noodle dish called Pad Thai. There are soups, stir frys and rice dishes too. At the end of your meal, you are given a slice of orange to sweeten your palate. With glass table tops, fresh flowers and eager-to-please servers, Sawasdee (meaning "hello, how are you?") is a restaurant that sparkles.

124. SHALLOS ANTIQUE RESTAURANT & BREWHOUSE

8811 Hardegan Street (County Line Mall)
Indianapolis, IN 46227
(317) 882-7997
Open daily for lunch & dinner.
Credit cards accepted.

A variety of beers and an eclectic mix of Indianapolis memorabilia are what draws people to Shallos, which proudly claims to be "the midwest's largest purveyor of rare and exotic beers!" Yes, there are over 500 beer choices—40 on draft, both imported and microbrewed. A collection of bottles and at least 300 tap handles border the upstairs and downstairs walls, accented with pictures of historical significance to Hoosiers: Polar Ice & Fuel, Indianapolis Brewing Company, 1930-1940 IU vs Purdue football programs, and L.S. Ayres tearoom, to name a few. There is also a 38-star U.S. flag, a "Smoke Room" window from the Gunn Hotel, and lots more. The menu cover carries out the antique theme when it boldly advertises "Air Conditioned and Ice Water!" A variety of appetizers and sandwiches fill the menu, along with full dinner entrees. Try your main course "swamped," a Caribbean marinade specialty.

125. SHAPIRO'S DELICATESSEN

808 South Meridian Street
Indianapolis, IN 46225
(317) 631-4041
Open daily for breakfast, lunch & dinner.
Credit cards accepted.

Established in 1905, Shapiro's is considered to be one of the ten "ultimate delis" in the country, and its roots are right here in Indianapolis. Now in its fourth generation, today's staff treats every day as if it were opening day, witnessed by those going through the line and seeing the enthusiasm of the servers. There's often a moment of panic when you see all the tantalizing choices. After deciding what you want, put on blinders so you aren't tempted to try something else! The desserts come first and the pies, baked in-house, are almost impossible to pass by. The sandwiches are next: corned beef, pastrami, peppered beef, brisket, summer sausage, and chopped liver, all served on rye bread or egg bun with or without a dill pickle. If you got by that station, you can choose one of the plate meals: stuffed pepper or cabbage, beef burger with grilled onions, meat loaf or chicken. The complete meal comes with two sides: macaroni and cheese, baked beans, green beans or noodles. At this point, you take a deep breath, sit down at one of the many tables, and savor every delicious bite.

126. SHELBI STREET CAFE & BISTRO

1105 Shelby Street
Indianapolis, IN 46203
(317) 687-4857
Open Monday-Saturday for continental breakfast & lunch;
Wednesday-Saturday for dinner. Closed Sunday.
Credit cards accepted.

Located in Fountain Square, this bright, contemporary cafe with its casual atmosphere is a great spot to enjoy a meal while visiting the historic neighborhood. Coffee and pastries are available early morning. The lunch menu features unique salads, sandwiches on homemade bread, gourmet pizzas and pastas, with an additional variety of appetizers and entrees on the dinner menu. Grilled pork loin with raspberry chipotle sauce and blue cheese is a favorite choice, along with a marinated and grilled yellow fin tuna with black bean and corn salsa. Seasonal outdoor dining is also available at the Rooftop Garden where you can relax and enjoy your meal while watching the sunset and a spectacular 360-degree view of downtown Indianapolis and beyond.

127. SLIPPERY NOODLE INN

372 South Meridian Street
Indianapolis, IN 46225
(317) 631-6968
Open Monday-Saturday for lunch & dinner;
Sunday for dinner.
Credit cards accepted.

The Slippery Noodle has quite a colorful history both above and below the ground. Established in 1850, it is listed in the National Register of Historic Places and is believed to be the oldest commercial building left standing in Indianapolis. Located close to the train station, it was originally built as a road house and bar for railroad passengers, became a way station for the Underground Railroad during the Civil War, and even housed a bordello which operated until 1953. Today, the "Noodle's" claim to fame is the Live Blues Bands featured seven nights a week. Patrons enjoy grabbing a bite to eat from a variety of sandwich, sub, snack and dinner choices while listening to music and absorbing the history of this Indiana "landmark."

128. SOME GUYS PIZZA-PASTA-GRILL

6235 Allisonville Road
Indianapolis, IN 46220
(317) 257-1364
Open Tuesday-Friday for lunch;
Tuesday-Sunday for dinner. Closed Monday.
Credit cards accepted.

A neighborhood gathering place for years, Some Guys is a comfortable family spot that has withstood the test of time. Bruce Dean's expression of "Some Guys...it's an art" is presented in paintings and murals that decorate the walls of each booth. Wood-fired pizza got its start here in Indianapolis with Santa Fe, Jamaican, BBQ Chicken and Greek pizza among the specialties. You can design your own pizza or choose the traditional or vegetarian. For those who are not pizza hungry, there are salads, woodoven pasta dishes and sandwiches. The first weekend of the month is "Lasagna Weekend."

129. TASTE CAFÉ & MARKETPLACE

5164 North College Avenue
Indianapolis, IN 46205
(317) 925-2233
Open daily for breakfast & lunch.
Credit cards accepted.

Creative combinations of ingredients is what makes dining at "Taste" a pleasurable experience. Imagine breakfast choices of bagels with peanut butter and jelly, a granola parfait, or a "c.b.&g.," which is cheddar, biscuits and gravy. For lunch, a mouth-watering array of wonderfully colorful and tasty salads are displayed in the food cases. Pick a salad or two, a sandwich like curried chicken salad, B.A.L.T. where "A" is for avocado, or roast turkey and smoked bacon. Once you've had a side of french fries, you will come back for more! Desserts abound: hummingbird cake, bread pudding, chocolate cupcakes and more. It's truly a "Taste" treat to dine at this restaurant.

130. THREE SISTERS CAFÉ & BAKERY

6360 North Guilford Avenue
Indianapolis, IN 46220
(317) 257-5556
Open daily for breakfast & lunch.
Credit cards accepted.

The name of this establishment and the food served embodies an Iroquois tradition that is hundreds of years old: "Food is sacred and enjoyment of it with friends is a gift." The seasonal, mostly vegetarian menu honors the belief that these gifts come to us from nature. The "three sisters" are corn, beans and squash: the corn and beans are planted together in a mound and the corn stalk provides a trellis for the winding bean plant; the squash is planted in between to fight off the weeds and help maintain moisture in the soil. You'll enjoy the breakfast choices of eggs with numerous veg-etable combinations, griddle cakes and breads plus the popular powerhouse potatoes. Lunch features a delightful assortment of soups, sandwiches and salads. Entrees include a black bean meatloaf, grilled salmon filet, citrus marinated tilapia, and noodles with your choice of pastas and sauces, all prepared with the freshest food possible.

131. VITO PROVOLONE'S

8031 South Meridian Street
Indianapolis, IN 46217
(317) 888-1112
Open daily for dinner.
Credit cards accepted.

A red-headed Italian owns this restaurant, named after his grandfather Vito who is pictured in various places throughout the dining areas. Wine bottles filled with flowers decorate the tables; wine bottles filled with wine decorate the shelves. Dine in this casual atmosphere offering gourmet pizzas with names abbreviating the ingredients, such as S.M.O.G. (sausage, mushroom, onions, green peppers), B.O.T. (bacon, onion, tomatoes), or try a stuffed spinach, Greek or seafood pizza. You can "build your own pasta" dish or enjoy chicken, beef or seafood prepared in a special Italian way. The menu tells the guest that "the PASTA-bilities are endless!!"

132. YATS

5303 North College
Indianapolis, IN 46220
(317) 253-8817
Open daily for lunch & dinner.
Cash, check or debit card accepted.

Joe claims that his place is for "Yats," people who love good food--"a Yat keeps livin' to eat." No frills with this restaurant. Order at the counter--samples are offered if you aren't sure what you want. The menu is Cajun, the flavors are spicy, and the number of choices is manageable. There are always vegetarian options along with gumbo, jambalaya, pazole stew, red beans, sausage and rice. All dishes are the same price. If you can't decide what you would like, you may order half of one entree and half of another! The menu may change, but tasting is always an option.

133. SONDY'S SYCAMORE GRILLE

113 West Sycamore
Kokomo, IN 46901
(765) 457-2220
Open Monday-Saturday for lunch & dinner. Closed Sunday.
Credit cards accepted.

There's a list of interesting and historical "things to see" while visiting this restaurant: doors and glass panels from churches and Indiana mansions; paper mache bird heads that were helmets worn in the Chicago Civic Opera in 1925; an old banker's table in the bar from the Howard County Bank; and much more! A life-size Blues Brothers statue greets you at the entrance. You can dine in the bar with its lively decor and atmosphere, or in the dining room, which is more sedate. In addition to the house favorites of coconut shrimp appetizer, pork BBQ, teriyaki chicken and veggie stir fry, the menu is filled with steak, seafood (the nutty grouper is recommended), chicken and pasta choices. For lunch or a lighter appetite at dinner, a variety of soups, salads and sandwiches are also available.

134. BRUNO'S

212 Brown Street
West Lafayette, IN 47106
(765) 743-1668
Open daily for dinner.
Credit cards accepted.

A well-known landmark to Boilermaker fans, this Swiss Italian restaurant is filled with memorabilia! The walls tell stories about local athletes who have gone on to play professionally. In fact, Bob Griese and Len Dawson are among the famous visitors! The pizza kitchen is in plain view as you enter the restaurant, and the pizza is still unbeatable. Bruno Dough is the recommended appetizer--golf ball size pieces of deep-fried pizza dough, brushed with garlic butter and served with meat or cheese sauce. Homemade lasagna, pasta dinners, and a variety of veal, pork and chicken dishes round out the Italian menu. The Swiss influence can be found in choices of wiener schnitzel, cheese fondue, bratwurst and knackwurst. Interestingly, catfish has also become a favorite at this restaurant.

135. MAIZE An American Grill

112 North 3rd Street
Lafayette, IN 47901
(765) 429-6125
Open Monday-Saturday for dinner. Closed Sunday.
Credit cards accepted.

Located in a renovated building just across the street from the Tippecanoe County Courthouse, this inviting restaurant beckons you to sit down and enjoy a meal. A large, winding bar is the focal point of the comfortable dining area with brick walls, high ceiling and a small balcony. Mouth-watering menu selections include creatively prepared salads such as one with mixed greens, blue cheese, pecans and apples. Enticing entrees like farafelle pasta, pecan-crusted catfish, veal liver, blue cheese crusted steak, and rotisserie duck and chicken are just a few of the outstanding choices. This is "midwest food with a flair!"

136. MCGRAW'S STEAK, CHOP & FISH HOUSE

2707 South River Road
West Lafayette, IN 47906
(765) 743-3932
Open Tuesday-Saturday for dinner. Closed Sunday & Monday.
Credit cards accepted.

As you wind down South River Road, a lighted fishing boat marks the place to turn into this establishment. It is close to Fort Ouiatenon. The catfish on the menu is the only evidence of what used to be called Stiney's Restaurant. Today, there is an inviting atmosphere with a brightly polished wood floor, comfortable bar, and a tantalizing menu. Appetizers vary from fried shoestring onions to poached shrimp martinis. Salad choices include the black and blue steak and fall harvest salad. Tempting entrees feature great steaks, sauteed walleye, baked honey mustard salmon or chicken McGraw. A "Dining Secrets" reader reported that the prime rib special is "uniquely different and out of sight!"

137. SARAH'S OAKS

4545 West 660 South
Lafayette, IN 47909
(765) 538-3880
RESERVATIONS ONLY.
Open Wednesday-Saturday for breakfast,
lunch & dinner. Closed Sunday-Tuesday.
Cash or checks accepted.

Located nine miles southwest of Lafayette (across the street from the Quaker meeting house in the Farmers Institute Community), this restored 1860 Quaker home is the setting for a special dining experience. Meals are served family style in your own room, lighted by a kerosene lamp. There is no set menu but suggested main courses include pan-fried chicken, pot roast, baked pork chops, roast pork loin and baked steak. Lunch is usually a casserole. Appropriate sides, salads, and homemade bread and desserts are served with all meals. An old-fashioned flower and butterfly garden are on the grounds. The restaurant can accommodate 34 people and is available for private parties. (48 hours advance reservations are required and a minimum of six guests.)

138. TRIPLE XXX RESTAURANT
2 North Salisbury Street
West Lafayette, IN 47906
(765) 743-5373
Open daily for breakfast, lunch & dinner.
Cash only establishment.

When a restaurant has been around for almost 80 years, it is worth a visit to see why it is special. The literature says "our name may be XXX, but our food is rated G." Burgers are called "chop steaks," 100% sirloin, "always fresh, never frozen." They make their own pork BBQ, grilled tenderloins, chili, and potato salad. Then there's the root beer: Triple XXX, one of a few independent brands left. The story actually began in a Galveston, Texas brewery in 1895 and the timeline moves from beer to soft drinks to Triple XXX "thirst stations" (root beer drive-ins). In the restaurant, this historical root beer is served in a frosty glass or in a float, but it can be purchased in bottles that suggest it "makes thirst a joy." Being close to Purdue University, the gold and black sundae (butterscoth and hot fudge) is appropriate!

139. BIJOU
111 West Main Street (On the Square)
Lebanon, IN 46052
(765) 482-7090
Open Tuesday-Saturday for dinner. Closed Sunday & Monday.
Credit cards accepted.

Located on the square in view of the Boone County Courthouse, the hard work and enthusiasm of the husband (host)-wife (chef) team make dining here a pleasure. A building that previously housed a furniture store and insurance agency has been beautifully transformed into a comfortable, upscale restaurant. The crisp white table-cloths are a striking contrast to the rich taupe-colored walls and dark wood trim. The seasonal menu reflects a continental cuisine in the French tradition. The specialties are duck breast with Grand Marnier glaze and lamb loin chops, but the seafood is also outstanding! La Buvette (the Taproom) has a menu all its own with entrees of chicken breast Mornay, lite salads, and filet mignon, along with snacks, soups, salads and appetizers.

140. HOSTESS HOUSE

723 West Fourth Street
Marion, IN 46953
(765) 664-3755
Open Monday-Friday for lunch;
evenings & weekends for private parties only.
Credit cards accepted.

The Hostess House is referred to as a "gracious historic landmark, cultural and civic gathering place." Built in 1912 by a wealthy Marion banker as a wedding gift to his bride, the mansion was the site of many cocktail parties, dinners and afternoon teas. Unfortunately, it was abandoned and vandalized in the 1940's, but a group of community-minded women refurbished the home and it now offers the Marion area a place for entertaining. It is often used for weddings, receptions, meetings and social gatherings. Being open to the public for lunch offers visitors the pleasure of eating on the sun porch, in the elegant dining room with a huge round table, or in other rooms of the beautifully appointed home. The menu includes a variety of sandwiches, salads and extraordinary desserts!

141. HEARTHSTONE RESTAURANT

18149 US Highway 52
Metamora, IN 47030
(765) 647-5204
Open daily for lunch & dinner.
Credit cards accepted.

Located in a quaint little town with over 100 craft shops, a grist mill, riverboat and railroad, the Hearthstone is a well-known landmark at the edge of town. Casual dining is offered in a country atmosphere—you can relax on the porch overlooking the canal, or enjoy your meal inside by the huge stone fireplace. Popular menu items served all day include pan-fried chicken, country cured ham, catfish and charbroiled steaks. A buffet is available Friday through Sunday. Everything is made from scratch, including wonderful biscuits and pies. Recognized in Midwest Living magazine.

142. ZYDECO CAJUN RESTAURANT

11 East Main Street
Mooresville, IN 46158
(317) 834-3900
Open Friday & Saturday for lunch; Thursday-Saturday for dinner.
Closed Sunday & Monday.
Credit cards accepted.

The owners wanted to bring the tastes of South Louisiana to Central Indiana and they've done that and lots more! It is Mardi Gras every day at Zydeco's and you will immediately get caught up in the celebration. There are streamers, twinkling lights, beads, jesters, and bold colors everywhere! The most exciting menu items are Cajun. A hearty choice of appetizers includes Crescent City boiled shrimp, oysters, tasso (highly seasoned smoked pork), and frog legs. Salads and soups--gumbo ya-ya, jambalaya, red beans and rice--are popular choices, along with Cajun entrees smothered in a thick, flavorful sauce termed "etouffee." The menu changes seasonally, and spring is the time for the crawfish boil. Specialty drinks are also available.

143. KOPPER KETTLE INN
US Route 52
Morristown, IN 46161
(765) 763-6767
Open Tuesday-Sunday for lunch & dinner. Closed Monday.
Credit cards accepted.

In business since 1923, the Kopper Kettle has a delightfully restful atmosphere where you can savor their famous Hoosier fried chicken, broiled prime steaks and delicious seafood, served family-style. The large house is a veritable art museum, displaying a fascinating collection of art objects from many parts of the world. From the beautiful antique furnishings and artifacts to the balconies, fountains and strolling gardens, the Kopper Kettle has a distinctive charm unmatched by the finest European restaurants.

144. VERA MAE'S BISTRO
209 South Walnut Street
Muncie, IN 47305
(765) 747-4941
Open Monday-Friday for lunch & dinner;
Saturday for dinner. Closed Sunday.
Credit cards accepted.

As you enter this storefront restaurant, you know you are someplace special. The atmosphere is comfortably inviting and the decor has a similar warmth with seasonal ornaments hanging from tree branches. Relax in the full lounge or at the bar that originally served patrons at grandmother Vera's diner and enjoy piano music and jazz on Thursday, Friday and Saturday evenings. A wide variety of lunch choices include quiche, turkey foccacia, grilled reuben or chicken curry melt. If you're interested in hor d'oeuvres before dinner, try the baked brie or seafood al forno. Dinner entrees are equally imaginative with pistachio crusted filet and chicken brie raspberry among the selections. Of course, you must save room for dessert: bread pudding with whiskey sauce, Cabernet pear tarte, or coconut macadamia nut tarte.

145. ALEXANDER'S ON THE SQUARE
864 Logan Street
Noblesville, IN 46060
(317) 773-9177
Open daily.
Credit cards accepted.

Choose from 36 flavors of Velvet Ice Cream, then decide if you want a sundae, old fashioned soda, malt, shake, Stewart root beer float (in a jar if you like), cone or dish! Relax and enjoy your treat in the ice cream parlor while looking at the wall decorations of old food and can labels, reminding patrons that this space was once a grocery store. Or you might choose to eat your ice cream as you walk around the Noblesville Square, view the fine architecture of the old court house, peek in the shops, or listen to the entertainment on a summer weekend. By the way, Alexander's does invite you to have lunch before your ice cream! The menu is filled with a nice selection of salads, soups, chili, sandwiches, wraps and munchies.

146. ASIAN GRILL
74 North 9th Street
Noblesville, IN 46060
(317) 773-9990
Open Monday-Saturday for lunch & dinner. Closed Sunday.
Credit cards accepted.

Housed on the square in Noblesville, the late 1800's store has been redesigned to showcase the original wood floors while at the same time looking sleek and contemporary. Asian Grill serves unique cuisines from Cambodia, China, India, Japan, Thailand and Vietnam. In addition to traditional appetizers, there is Vegetable Samosa, a pastry filled with potatoes and mixed vegetables with a mango and mint chutney, and a Vegetable Pakora, a combination of chopped onions, lentil flour, coconut, cashew nuts and spices with mint chutney. The entrees are another story! Once you decide between chicken, beef, seafood, vegetarian or noodles, you then begin the difficult task of choosing which combination of vegetable and spices sounds the best to you! Asian beers and wines from many lands are available to complement your meal.

147. CLASSIC KITCHEN
610 Hannibal Street
Noblesville, IN 46060
(317) 773-7385
Open Tuesday-Saturday for lunch; Friday & Saturday for dinner.
Closed Sunday & Monday.
Credit cards accepted.

Located just south of the courthouse in Noblesville, this marvelous restaurant offers fine dining in a light and airy French-style setting. Gourmet magazine calls the fare "eclectic geographic" which is a reflection of the extensive travels of the chef/proprietor. All entrees are prepared in house with quality, healthy products—no additives or preservatives are used. The lunch menu features homemade soups, quiche, whole wheat crepes, and their own natural ice creams with vanilla short-breads. Candlelight dinners on Friday and Saturday nights include classic specialties of veal, chicken, fish and vegetables, plus a changing repertoire of French and Belgian chocolate desserts. Reservations are requested.

148. EDDIE'S CORNER CAFÉ
101 North Tenth Street
Noblesville, IN 46060
(317) 776-9935
Open Monday-Saturday for lunch & dinner; Sunday for lunch.
Credit cards accepted.

A small sign reads, "People have eaten here and left perfectly normal." Eddie creates a family friendly atmosphere by wandering among the tables and chatting with patrons, making the diner feel "better than normal." The walls tell stories about Eddie's interests and his life. There are walls of fame, sports and entertainment, but of special significance is the Nicaraguan Mission story on the back wall. People of all ages gather here to eat the daily special or a selection from the menu--soup, salad, a curly Q hot dog, sub sandwich or southwest chili are the popular choices. Daughter Sandra makes all the homemade desserts!

149. THE HAMILTON RESTAURANT
933 Conner Street
Noblesville, IN 46060
(317) 770-4545
Open Monday-Saturday for lunch; Wednesday-Saturday for dinner.
Closed Sunday.
Credit cards accepted.

In view of the county courthouse, The Hamilton Restaurant advertises "upscale dining in a casual atmosphere." Paintings by local artists decorate the interior. The chef/owner takes pride in preparing contemporary American cuisine with a menu that reflects the foods of the seasons. For lunch there are sandwiches, including a hot brown, salads and entrees featuring grilled salmon, chicken, or skewered shrimp. Dinner choices may begin with baked brie, smoked salmon with grated potato cake, or another tasty appetizer. Served with vegetables and soup or house salad, innovatively prepared main courses include steak, bacon wrapped pork, stuffed chicken breast, and various seafood selections. In addition to the entrees, dinner-size salads are offered. Your server can also recommend the perfect wine to accompany your meal. Different homemade desserts are available every day; in fact, you can view them in the cases as you enter the restaurant so you can plan ahead to save room!

150. BONGE'S TAVERN
9830 West 280N
Perkinsville, IN 46011
(765) 734-1625
Open Tuesday-Saturday for dinner. Closed Sunday & Monday.
Credit cards accepted.

Bonge's Tavern put this small town on the map as people literally flock to Perkinsville to eat in this old converted hardware store. You might have to wait on the porch or outdoors if the weather is nice, but it is well worth the trip. The owner takes pride in the rustic-style restaurant he has created and recommends you take a look at the memorabilia displayed throughout, including the pinball machine tops hanging on the wall in the private dining area. The menu changes regularly and there is a variety of blackboard specials, but the popular Perkinsville pork is always on the menu. Some who visit Bonge's restrooms write a message on the wall. Be sure to check it out!

151. SIDING BY THE TRACKS

8 West 10th Street (Downtown)
Peru, IN 46970
(765) 473-4041
Open Tuesday-Friday for lunch & dinner; Saturday for dinner;
Sunday for brunch. Closed Monday.
Credit cards accepted.

Train buffs will love dining in one of two restored railroad cars or in a dining room embellished with antiques and train memorabilia. In fact, the owner calls himself a "railroad junkie!" Both a lunch buffet and smaller dinner buffet are available or you can order off the menu, except on Friday when diners come to feast on the popular seafood buffet. The food is described as "home cooking with a gourmet touch." There is also a brunch on Sunday featuring a wonderful variety of homemade pastries. Steaks and seafood are the house specialty, and outstanding desserts include Kahlua ice cream pie and homemade cheesecakes.

152. FRANK AND MARY'S CATFISH HOUSE

Pittsboro, IN 46167
(317) 892-3485
Open daily for lunch & dinner.
Credit cards accepted.

Originating in 1945 when rationing ended after World War II, Frank and Mary's is truly an institution. Five generations of Herrings have been involved in the business, which began with beer and codfish sandwiches and is now known as "the place to eat catfish." You don't need an address; just go to the main street in Pittsboro and all the cars will tell you that you've found the right place for a great catfish sandwich or dinner. There are other seafood entrees on the menu, such as frog legs, codfish and shrimp, and landlubbers can choose from hamburgers, tenderloins and steaks. Daily lunch specials are also available, but the catfish is the specialty every day!

153. OLDE RICHMOND INN

138 South Fifth Street
Richmond, IN 47374
(765) 962-2247
Open daily for lunch & dinner.
Credit cards accepted.

Located in the old Richmond area, this former 1892 residence exhibits the work of local "south-end Dutch" wood craftsmen and masons. The Victorian setting is accented with Italian decorative tiles, a stained glass wall from the 1800's, and stained glass fixtures designed by Richmond and Cincinnati craftsmen. A unique chandelier from the home of Micajah Henley, the inventor of roller skates, lights the north dining room and three fireplaces add to the warm and inviting atmosphere. Special meals are prepared daily and served in a gracious and professional manner. To whet the appetite, sample the shrimp bianca appetizer, a house specialty. The American and continental-style menu offers a variety of prime cut steaks, seafood, chicken and pasta entrees for dinner; salads, sandwich platters and chef's casserole of the day for lunch; and many daily blackboard specials. There is seasonal al fresco dining on the patio, and on-site banquet facilities are available for private parties.

154. ROD AND GUN STEAKHOUSE
2525 East Lambert
Rosedale, IN 47874
(812) 466-2521
Open Tuesday-Saturday for dinner. Closed Sunday & Monday.
Credit cards accepted.

The restaurant dates back to the roaring 20's when, as part of a local farm, it was offered as the stakes in a gambling game. Eleven-year-old Bob Johnson was hired by the new owner and became a very dedicated employee. Over the years there was a fire and then another change in ownership, but in 1975, Bob Johnson did what he thought was impossible: he bought the restaurant, which his son continues to operate today. There are no cards or dice around and the roulette wheel is silent, but the intimate dining areas carry on the tradition and the story. Of course, steaks are the specialty with a 20-ounce porterhouse leading the list. Chicken and seafood are also available.

155. RED ONION
3901 West State Road 47
Sheridan, IN 46069
(317) 758-0424
Open daily for lunch & dinner.
Credit cards accepted.

The owners of this small town restaurant pride themselves on great food served in a comfortable, casual atmosphere that draws patrons from all over the Central Indiana area. In fact, about 95% of their customers are from out of town. They are best known for the breaded tenderloin, hand-cut daily and served on a 7" round bun, but those who have eaten there believe it's at least a 10" bun! All of the sandwiches are large and cater to a hearty appetite, but feel free to split one with a friend. Popular dinner items include hand-cut steaks, all you can eat catfish on Thursdays, and prime rib dinners on the weekends.

156. DAWSON'S ON MAIN
1464 Main Street
Speedway, IN 46224
(317) 247-7000
Open daily for lunch & dinner.
Credit cards accepted.

The menu encourages diners to "race on in" and yes, this delightful restaurant sits on a corner just one block from the Indianapolis Motor Speedway. There's a friendly neighborhood atmosphere with umbrellas over tables outside and an inviting, brick-walled, booth-lined dining room inside. The lunch fare features appetizers, salads, soups, sandwiches and entrees. The "D" on the menu designates house specialties like spinach and artichoke dip, iceberg wedge with apple hickory bacon and honey roasted pecans, signature mushroom soup, flat iron sirloin, and Chef Hef's Moby Dick sandwich. For dinner, there is an outstanding selection of steak and seafood entrees plus smoked baby back ribs, a peppercorn crusted pork loin, and Creole chicken.

157. MUG N BUN
5211 West 10th Street
Speedway, IN 46224
(317) 247-9186
Open daily for lunch & dinner.
Cash only establishment.

Take a step back and enjoy reliving the past at this well-known, west side drive-in that has been a fixture in Speedway for almost 50 years. Turn on your headlights or press a button on the picnic table and a waitress will appear to take your order! The Mug N Bun is an independent root beer maker with a brew that is full-bodied, tangy and served in a frosted mug. You can enjoy a breaded tenderloin, BBQ sandwich, hamburger, hand-dipped onion rings that are cut fresh daily, root beer float or other drive-in specialties, but several items stand out as being unique: mini corndogs, sweet potato fries with sugar and cinnamon, and delicious fried apple crescents.

158. THE BUSH
932 Locust Street
Terre Haute, IN 47807
(812) 238-1148
Open Monday-Saturday for lunch & dinner. Closed Sunday.
Credit cards accepted.

The "lure" of this restaurant is the cod fish sandwiches! Located next to the railroad tracks, the local people have been gathering in the bar and dining room for over 50 years, well-documented by the photos on the walls. Look for the pictures of Howdy Doody & Bob and Hopalong Cassidy! The breading for the cod and the tenderloin is homemade and delicious. You can order a baby or jumbo fish sandwich (one or two pieces), and the tenderloin whole or half with sides of 'shrooms, rings, cole slaw, French fries, or hush puppies. Pasta, salad, burgers, chicken, ribeye steak and catfish are also available, but cod is the specialty.

159. GERHARDT'S BIERSTUBE RESTAURANT
1724 Lafayette Avenue
Terre Haute, IN 47804
(812) 466-9249
Open Tuesday-Friday for lunch & dinner;
Saturday for dinner. Closed Sunday & Monday.
Credit cards accepted.

As you step inside and hear the music in the background, then glance around at the lace curtains, wood carvings, and beer steins, you will feel as if you're in a restaurant in Germany, certainly not in Terre Haute! Gerhardt purchased the restaurant from a German immigrant in 1977 (her husband's ghost is still blamed for broken glasses and dishes.) The Bierstube has been known as a gathering place for many Germans. Sausages, reubens, and sauerbraten with sides of potato salad, sauerkraut, red cabbage, spaetzle or pickled beets are on the lunch menu. For dinner, Schnitzels, Kassler Rippchen (smoked pork chop), and Weinerschnitzel are the specialties. It's hard to pass up the apfelstrudel or the Heidelberg Haus Torte for dessert. "Gut essen und trinken half leib und seele zusammen" (good eating and drinking keep body and soul together).

160. M. MOGGER'S BREWERY EATERY & PUB
908 Poplar Street
Terre Haute, IN 47802
(812) 234-9202
Open daily for lunch & dinner.
Credit cards accepted.

You'll take a trip into the past when you enter this old brewery named after Matthias Mogger, a German immigrant. The E. Bleemel Building, built in 1837, housed Mogger's Brewery from 1848-1868 and is a significant part of early beer brewing history in the Wabash Valley. The floors, woodwork and the dumb waiter that carried barrels from the basement to the store level, along with other brewing paraphernalia, create a unique atmosphere in which to dine. Today, Mogger's has over 170 beers to choose from and offers an MBA (Masters of Beer Appreciation)! There are many choices of burgers, sandwiches, steak, seafood, pork and pasta entrees, plus soups and salad dressings that are homemade. The Italian beef sandwich and the drunken cod are reported to be excellent.

161. PINO'S "IL SONETTO" RESTAURANT
4200 South 7th Street
Terre Haute, IN 47802
(812) 299-9255
Open Monday-Friday for lunch & dinner. Saturday & Sunday for dinner.
Credit cards accepted.

If you ever met Pino, you know he was a true artist: songwriter, inventor, poet, and chef. He lived in Sicily and worked in a pastry shop from second grade until he came to the United States in 1960. Through hard work and savings, he opened a successful restaurant and pizzeria in Brooklyn. When Pino moved to Indiana, his original plan was to retire, but he opened this restaurant instead! Pino's reputation continues through the three chefs he trained in the true Italian tradition. The cuisine is authentic and meals are cooked to order, featuring various pastas with a mouth-watering array of sauces, a complete selection of vegetarian dishes catering to the health conscious, and creatively prepared veal, chicken, meat and seafood entrees.

162. STABLES STEAKHOUSE
939 Poplar Street
Terre Haute, IN 47807
(812) 232-6677
Open Monday-Saturday for dinner. Closed Sunday.
Credit cards accepted.

The warm and inviting atmosphere of this restaurant creates the feeling that you are in a casual, well-renovated historic setting. Built in 1890 as a stable for the brewery across the street, the look has been preserved throughout the interior. There are horse stalls, high ceilings, barn paraphernalia, and horses decorating the furniture uphol-stery. The main fare is hand-cut steaks, but the menu also includes a one pound pork chop, chicken, fresh seafood, lobster and pasta. A wine cellar and well-stocked bar is available for your enjoyment. Banquet facilities and catering are available.

163. STOOKEY'S

125 East Main Street
Thorntown, IN 46071
(765) 436-7202
Open Tuesday-Saturday for lunch & dinner. Closed Sunday & Monday.
Credit cards accepted.

If you mention "catfish" to "Dining Secrets" readers, many will respond, "Have you been to Stookey's?" In the small town of Thorntown, just north of Indianapolis, you will find great catfish, a tasty ribeye steak and "out-of-this-world" onion rings. The Stookey family opened and operated the restaurant starting in 1975. The current owners are committed to the Stookey name and are dedicated to upholding the restaurant's fine reputation. Race fans will appreciate the "500" decor in the bar.

164. IVANHOE'S

979 South Main Street
Upland, IN 46989
(765) 998-7261
Open daily for lunch & dinner.
Credit cards accepted.

If you have a craving for delicious ice cream, you must stop at Ivanhoe's, but you'll have to choose from more than 100 different varieties available! Good old-fashioned hamburgers plus excellent salads are another good reason to stop here. Ivanhoe's started as a drive-in in the '60s and has grown into a large, popular place to eat. Forget the diet and watching the fat grams because this is worth it!

165. L.A. CAFÉ

4 South Main Street
Whitestown, IN 46075
(317) 769-7503
Open daily for lunch & dinner.
Credit cards accepted.

The motto is "Let the good times roll" and when "rolling" into this small town, stop at the place on Main Street where motorcycles are parked alongside a stretch limo! People from all walks of life are drawn to this eclectic "destination" restaurant. The inside is decorated in orange, black and chrome with motorcycle memorabilia every-where. The family-friendly atmosphere is accentuated by black napkins on white tablecloths covered with paper that children can color on while waiting for their meal. The menu begins with homemade soups, salads, and a "fiery" shrimp cocktail made with fresh horseradish. Entrees include hand-cut steaks, ribs, fresh fish, and daily seafood and pasta specials. The lunch menu features burgers, sandwiches, a "killer burrito," and various salads. The Cafe's signature desserts are the cheesecake with raspberry sauce, or a creme bruleé with chocolate-dipped strawberries. Beverages include a complete line of beer, wine and spirits.

166. BRiX ZIONSVILLE BISTRO
65 South First Street
Zionsville, IN 46077
(317) 732-2233
Open Tuesday-Friday for lunch & dinner; Saturday for dinner.
Closed Sunday & Monday.
Credit cards accepted.

Perhaps you have spent a day in Zionsville at the antique and specialty stores and now it's time to slow down, enjoy a glass of wine and look forward to a special meal at BRiX Zionsville Bistro. If weather permits, seating is available outside; otherwise, there are window seats in this bistro cafe. Their philosophy is to offer savory seasonal dishes with a focus on local products, making everything from scratch and made to order. Your mouth waters as you read the menu, from the appetizers to the entrees. A meal might start with sliced ahi tuna nicoise and BLT salad, followed by an inter-mezzo of house-made sorbet, and next, bourbon barbecued Mark Turner Farms ribs. Hopefully, you have saved room for the delectable desserts. Note that there is a "lighter side" lunch menu with special sandwiches, soups, salads and a quiche of the day.

167. TRADERS POINT CREAMERY CAFE
9101 Moore Road
Zionsville, IN 46077
(317) 733-1700 x25
Open Wednesday-Sunday for lunch & Dairy Bar; Saturday for dinner.
Friday for dinner during summer months.
Credit cards accepted.

It's hard to believe that this 100% grass-fed dairy in its idyllic surroundings is so easily accessible to I-465. Plan to visit the dairy and Green Market at mealtime and experience the pleasure of sampling the latest Traders Point Creamery products and eating a healthy meal. Dining takes place in a barn-like structure with fresh flowers on your table, and Saturday evening meals can be enjoyed in the candle-lit loft. Every effort is made to use certified organic ingredients in the salads, sandwiches and entrees. Appetizers include cheese and seasonally fresh fruit. Similarly, the already tasty desserts of flan, lemon tart and brownies can be embellished with ice cream, yogurt or fresh berries.

Southern Indiana

168. APPLEWOOD FOOD & SPIRITS
215 Judiciary Street
Aurora, IN 47001
(812) 926-1166
Open daily for lunch & dinner.
Credit cards accepted.

Built in the 1800's, this waterfront restaurant is nestled between two casino boats located in the area. Prints of old paddle boats decorate the walls. The restaurant has several levels, including a deck for outside dining, and music is played on Friday and Saturday nights. For lunch there are burgers, 14 different hot and cold sandwiches, soups and salads, and entrees such as liver and onions and beef or chicken stir fry. Dinner choices include chicken Applewood (pecans, apples, honey and brandy sauce), ribs, pork loin with pepper sauce, steaks, "Hillforest" pot roast served the old-fashioned way, plus seafood and specialty salads.

169. THE SHERMAN HOUSE
35 South Main Street
Batesville, IN 47006
(812) 934-2407; (800) 445-4939
Open daily for breakfast, lunch & dinner.
Credit cards accepted.

This popular inn has served as a landmark in the area since it opened in 1852. Decorated with pictures of General Sherman and renderings of art from the Civil War period, you can relax and unwind in the old-world atmosphere and enjoy some of the tastiest food in southern Indiana. The specialty is traditional German fare--wiener schnitzel, bratwurst and sauerbraten--but a nice selection of wonderful American dishes are featured as well.

170. GOLDEN GABLES RESTAURANT
Junction of Highway 37 South & Highway 50 West
Bedford, IN 47421
(812) 275-7371
Open 24 hours.
Cash only establishment.

You'll find this 50's diner tucked in next to a gas station at the spot where SR 50 and SR 37 intersect. Breakfast is available anytime during the day and the scratch sausage gravy over biscuits is the specialty. "Up and At 'Em" hotcakes, eggs and bacon, or the Down on the Farm are other good choices. If you would rather have lunch, you'll enjoy the 1950's-style sandwich platters (giant breaded tenderloin, pork BBQ, He-Man platter or the Big Gable platter) served with homemade coleslaw and old fashioned style French fries. Additional lunch and dinner items include country fried steak, breaded catfish filets, roast beef, and turkey or pork with gravy. The meals are good but the main attraction to Golden Gables is the pie--homemade cream pies with mile high meringue. Coconut cream is reportedly the most popular, but all the others are very tempting!

171. JANKO'S LITTLE ZAGREB
223 West 6th Street
Bloomington, IN 47404
(812) 332-0694
Open Monday-Saturday for dinner. Closed Sunday.
Credit cards accepted.

"Janko" is "Little Johnny" and Zagreb is the capital of Croatia. The restaurant's name commemorates John's grandmother who, as he was growing up, repeatedly talked about how much food people ate when they worked on the farms! The interior is decorated with red and white checked tablecloths, silverware wrapped in waxed paper, and posters on the walls. As you open the menu, you are informed that "all steaks are thick." Although the steaks are a specialty and superb, there is quite a variety of other choices, including barbecued ribs with a special hot sauce, thick juicy pork chops, meatballs Bucharest, Polish sausage and cabbage, Punjene paprika (stuffed pepper), eggplant, and additional taste treats!

172. LAUGHING PLANET CAFE
322 East Kirkwood Avenue (at Grant Street)
Bloomington, IN 47408
(812) 323-2233
Open daily for lunch & dinner.
Credit cards accepted.

The spicy aroma draws you into this restaurant that majors in "whole foods in a hurry." After you place your order at the counter, you can enjoy a hearty laugh as you peruse the walls: hanging bikes with the sign "Get a life get a bike," bold and colorful paintings, dinosaur toys, a shrine with customer messages asking for divine assistance, a framed original Swanson TV dinner tray, and much more! Nutritious burritos are the top sellers with a "How to Eat a Burrito" pictorial guide on each table. Burritos are stuffed with your choice of ingredients: veggies (including fresh leaf spinach, black bean hummus, broccoli, roasted potatoes, sweet corn), broiled chicken, cheeses, brown rice, pinto and black beans, guacamole, tofu, and sour cream (vegan available). Incredible homemade soups such as spinach lentil, Hungarian mushroom, and roasted garlic and potato are delicious. There are also salads and veggie burgers. You bus your own table and are encouraged not to be wasteful. You can indulge, though, in a chocolate chip or maple syrup and almond cookie!

173. ORIGINAL SCHOLARS INN GOURMET CAFE & WINE BAR

717 North College Avenue
Bloomington, IN 47404
(812) 323-1531
Open Tuesday-Friday for lunch & dinner; Saturday for dinner;
Sunday for brunch & dinner.
Credit cards accepted.

Housed in a 150-year-old mansion with Underground Railroad connections, the Scholars Inn provides gourmet dining in an "intellectual" atmosphere. Books are in full view, but the quotes printed along the molding on the ceiling are particularly interesting--"No poems can please long, nor live, which are written by water drinkers." Seating is available on the porch or upstairs in the vibrantly colorful, intimate dining room overseen by a woman painted on the ceiling! The lunch menu offers a selection of soups, salads, pastas and entrees. Perhaps you would choose the Scholar signature salad or Rocket salad with dried cherries, candied pecans, apples and champagne vinaigrette. The luncheon entrees vary from pine nut crusted salmon to handmade potato ravioli. The list of dinner appetizers is extensive and includes crispy calamari, crunchy crawfish, and bread with spreads sampler. There are several vegetarian entrees in addition to the fish du jour, citrus-teriyaki pork, beef and duck. Dessert is a must with peach kuchen, tiramisu, and berry martini as a few of the delectable choices!

174. RESTAURANT TALLENT

208 North Walnut Street
Bloomington, IN 47404
(812) 330-9801
Open Monday-Saturday for dinner. Closed Sunday.
Credit cards accepted.

Unless you lived in Bloomington years ago, you would never guess that this elegantly designed restaurant used to be the Ferris grocery store. Eye-catching art stands out on the chocolate covered walls, but the real focal point is the bar constructed of old wine bottle boxes. The chef labels the cuisine as "New American, emphasizing seasonal and regional ingredients while still using foie gras and truffles. There's a little French and Mediterranean, no soy, no fusion; BUT there's always grits from Oden!" The menu changes several times throughout the year and primarily reflects what is available in the Southern Indiana region during that season. Sweet corn soup and moules frites (basil pesto, and orange fennel dusted frites) are options for the first course. Some of the tempting main entrees include Fiedler Farms Pork Trio (white cheddar grits, braised kale, green tomato relish), wild salmon, Fischer Farms Ribeye with warm lemon and basil potato salad, and a Farmer's Market vegetable dish. Desserts are delightfully seasonal as well, from frozen blackberry parfait and blueberry tart to chocolate banana bread pudding and apple galette with caramel ice cream.

175. THE IRISH LION®

212 West 5th Street (Kirkwood)
Bloomington, IN 47404
(812) 336-9076
Open Monday-Saturday for lunch & dinner; Sunday for brunch & dinner.
Credit cards accepted.

This long, narrow tavern has been serving food and drink since 1882. The ice house out back, turn-of-the-century metal ceiling, and many antiques decorating the interior are all reminders of its earlier days. In Ireland, where no one point is more than 70 miles from the sea, a lot of seafood is consumed. Thus, after the customary drink to begin the meal, appetizers of shrimp, fresh oysters, mussels, clams, crab-heachain, oysters Rockefeller (an original recipe), or Blarney puff balls are offered. When you are ready for the main course, choose the corned beef and cabbage, Irish stew, rack of lamb, prime rib, lobster tail, shrimp, or perhaps the "rineanna"-- duckling half with apple-fennel bread stuffing. Then, top off your meal with a piece of apple walnut cake or whiskey pie! Irish soda bread is baked on site.

176. TROJAN HORSE

100 East Kirkwood Avenue (Walnut Street)
Bloomington, IN 47408
(812) 332-1101
Open daily for lunch & dinner.
Credit cards accepted.

As you approach the Trojan Horse, the "public view" kitchen entices passers-by to watch the lamb and beef being carved on the spit for the famous gyros. Inside, there is an IU flag and a Greek flag, suggesting that the menu is divided "Greek" and "American." Wonderful Greek appetizers include saganaki (flaming cheese) and dol-mas (grape leaves), while the American choices feature super fries (handcut with Walter's slicer), potato cakes, or grilled portabellos. In addition to gyros, souvlaki (marinated pork and fixings in a pita), a patty melt or tenderloin are offered. Zeus's recommendations for dinner include moussaka and other Greek specialties. If you're feeling indulgent, order the baklava, choclava or ambrosia for dessert. Visit the "Horse's Head Tavern" upstairs and look for the Medusa and Poseidon frescoes left over from the old nautical-themed restaurant.

177. UPTOWN CAFÉ

102 East Kirkwood Avenue
Bloomington, IN 47408
(812) 339-0900
Open Monday-Saturday for breakfast, lunch & dinner; Sunday for brunch.
Credit cards accepted.

Located just off the downtown square, this upscale café attracts a broad cross-section of people in this busy college town. The cuisine is described as "American food with attitude." Breakfast includes standard eggs the way you love them, and a few ways that might surprise you: potato cream cheese omelettes, eggs benedict, eggs sardou, and huevos rancheros. Lunch and dinner are a gumbo of flavors: big steaks, fresh fish, New Orleans favorites, etouffees and barbecued shrimp. Beer and wine are available, plus there's an espresso bar and soccer pub.

178. COLUMBUS BAR

322 Fourth Street
Columbus, IN 47201
(812) 375-8800
Open Monday-Saturday for lunch & dinner. Closed Sunday.
Credit cards accepted.

Originally a blacksmith shop built in 1890, this historic downtown landmark has been operating as a restaurant since the 1960's and many recall growing up and going to the "CB." Some of the historical aspects of the bar have been maintained, particularly the antique neon sign out front and the inviting horseshoe-shaped bar modeled after a streetcar. With the addition of their own microbrewery, you can enjoy fine handcrafted ales along with guest beers from around the world in the English-style pub. The private dining room offers a quieter, more relaxed environment and welcomes families with children. Menu highlights include the famous Columbus Tenderloin and Mile High Fish Sandwich, along with a reuben that has been hailed by many east coast guests as "authentic." Entrees like pork chops, chicken dinners and, of course, fish and chips are always available. Chef Nana makes special homemade soups, and they also make their own root beer and ice cream with unique weekly flavors, such as banana pancake and beer ice cream! This is a casual, friendly place to eat and mingle with the people of the community.

179. GARCIA'S MEXICAN RESTAURANT

3932 25th Street
Columbus, IN 47203
(812) 376-0783
Open Tuesday-Friday for lunch & dinner. Closed January-March.
Cash only establishment.

You'll find this family-owned restaurant tucked away in back of a small shopping center. As you step inside, you'll immediately notice the colorful and sparkling interior that creates a very inviting atmosphere. Comfortable seating is provided in alcoves of white stucco. Chips are served with both a sweet and hot sauce, a combination of flavors that tastefully complement each other. The menu is very straightforward with taco, enchilada and tostada combinations, along with burritos, chimichangas and chili relleno. There is a wonderful bean salad that can be combined with beef or chicken, and the guacamole adds another good flavor. This is a great place to go if you're in the mood for Mexican food!

180. TRE BICCHIERI

425 Washington Street
Columbus, IN 47201
(812) 372-1962
Open Tuesday-Saturday for lunch & dinner. Closed Sunday & Monday.
Credit cards accepted.

An invitation on the menu to "enter as strangers, leave as friends" gives you a good indication of how well you will be treated at this downtown restaurant. Tre Bicchieri ("three glasses" in Italian) is the story of three friends who combined their resources to make a dream come true. The chef is originally from Florida, thus the emphasis on seafood with an Italian twist: Bruschetta di Pesce, Ravioli Aragosta, Mussels Marinara, and Linguine di Mare. Additional choices include rosemary chicken, veal marsala, lasagna, and angry penne. Spumoni and cannoli are available for dessert or you might try the fried cheesecake or creme brulee. The Chef's Table can be reserved--a cozy spot separate from the main restaurant with a special view of the chefs in action and surrounded by pictures of family and friends. Be sure to look at the mural painted by local artist Nick Woolls.

181. TWIGS & SPRIGS TEAROOM

Stream Cliff Herb Farm & Winery
8225 S. County Road 90 W
Commiskey, IN 47227
(812) 346-5859
Open Wednesday-Sunday for lunch
from April to early October.
Candlelight dinners by reservation.
Credit cards accepted.

All of "Dining Secrets" criteria is present here: out-of-the-way location, history, people and food. Find Commiskey on the map, approach the town looking for a silo and greenhouse, then follow that line and you will find Stream Cliff Herb Farm. There is a 160-year history of the property and its development as Indiana's oldest herb farm. Today, there are multiple gardens depicting the pattern on a quilt, several old buildings, and a rustic tearoom sitting amongst the rows of flowers. The food incorporates the natural ingredients of the area, especially the herbs, and the serving plates are decorated with a colorful flower such as a nasturtium. For starters, there's a vegetable medley cheese soup. Follow it with a choice of dill and rosemary chicken or tuna salad, marjoram seafood salad, bird seed pasta salad, or a garden burger, turkey club or reuben sandwich. Dessert is a must with hummingbird cake at the top of the list. Afternoon country tea is served in keeping with the claim that "the taking of tea for a gardener is not a beverage, but a lifestyle." A winery has recently been established at the herb farm and customers can now enjoy a glass of wine in the tearoom.

182. MAGDALENA'S

103 East Chestnut Street
Corydon, IN 47112
(812) 738-8075
Open daily for lunch & dinner.
Credit cards accepted.

This restaurant is named after the owner's grandmother who brought many traditions with her when she arrived in the U.S. from southern Poland in 1920. You'll find a commitment to continuing these traditions in the food, service and charming setting. From its humble beginnings in 1991 as an ice cream shoppe, Magdalena's is now a full-service restaurant with banquet facilities and a gourmet gift shop where you can enjoy a cup of coffee. The menu states, "Life is uncertain, so eat dessert first" and you'll find a tempting selection of desserts listed first on the menu: hot apple dumpling, peanut butter pie, or bumbleberry pie (spiced apples, rhubarb, blackberries and raspberries)! Appetizers, homestyle soups served in bread bowls, sensational salads, lunch entrees and sandwiches are on the luncheon menu. Dinner selections feature seafood, classic chicken dishes, pasta, steaks and chops.

183. DILEGGE'S RESTAURANT

607 North Main
Evansville, IN 47711
(812) 428-3004
Open Monday-Friday for lunch & dinner; Saturday for dinner. Closed Sunday.
Credit cards accepted.

With ancestors from Italy, this family-owned restaurant guarantees superb Italian cuisine, specializing in all homemade sauces and desserts. The menu also includes a nice selection of chicken, beef, seafood, veal and pasta dishes. Surrounded by many beautiful plants and photos of flowers, you will enjoy dining in this casual, relaxed atmosphere.

184. DOGTOWN TAVERN

6201 Old Henderson Road
Evansville, IN 47712
(812) 423-0808
Open Tuesday-Sunday for lunch & dinner.
Closed Monday.
Credit cards accepted.

Built over 100 years ago to house the Cypress Post Office and saloon, the Dogtown Tavern is located close to the Ohio River. Reportedly, the name is attributed to the fact that hunters would gather with their dogs outside the saloon before taking off on a day's hunt through the fields and riverbanks. When you visit today, it is likely you will see a table of local people who come to the tavern for some good home cooking and some spirited conversation. The menu is similar to others you've seen. But, if you look carefully, you will find some yummy homemade and unique entries. Along with the sweet/sour slaw, Kate's potato, mashed with bacon and pickles, is a real treat. The "Dogtown Through the Garden" pizza is topped with cheese, beef, sausage, pepperoni, mushrooms, onion, green pepper, tomato and egg. Catfish fiddlers, farm raised and filleted, are the best sellers on the menu. Very little is new in the tavern, including the fans run by pulleys, and the food is just like mom used to make.

185. GERST BAVARIAN HAUS

2100 West Franklin Street
Evansville, IN 47712
(812) 424-1420
Open daily for lunch & dinner.
Credit cards accepted.

The Gerst Brewing Company opened in Nashville, Tennessee, in 1890 and flourished for many years, winning awards for its beers. When the brewery closed, a restaurant evolved but was also closed when the Tennessee Titans football stadium was constructed on the site. The owners of this restaurant relocated to Evansville and took over the space of the Heldt and Voelker hardware store, a building that was considered to be a prime example of turn of the century architecture. The windows still carry the hardware store advertisements, but inside you feel like you are in a German beer hall, complete with high ceilings, red and white checked tablecloths, flags and music. American food items are on the menu, but the main focus is German: potato pancakes, sauerkraut, bratwurst, knackwurst, schnitzels, sauerbraten, goulash, and the world famous Gerst Kasseler Rippchen (one-pound smoked pork chop!). There are 20 draft beers and 130 bottled beers from over 25 countries available.

186. HILLTOP INN
1100 Harmony Way
Evansville, IN 47720
(812) 422-1757
Open Monday-Saturday for lunch & dinner. Closed Sunday.
Credit cards accepted.

Built in 1839, this restaurant was originally an old saloon and stage coach stop. Located high on a hill just two miles from the Ohio River, it was a popular stop for weary travelers. It has maintained a very rustic, country atmosphere and features a 75-100 year old back bar. Hilltop offers your basic down home country cookin'—fried chicken, steaks and fiddlers—but if you're the more adventuresome type, you must try the brain sandwich, an unusual but popular menu item!

187. HOUSE OF COMO
2700 South Kentucky Avenue (Highway 41 South)
Evansville, IN 47714
(812) 422-0572
Open Tuesday-Saturday for dinner. Closed Sunday & Monday.
Cash or checks accepted.

Many consider this the best restaurant in Evansville, and comments made by the founder several years ago confirm that: "I don't need any advertising. I have all the business I can handle!" The restaurant is in an unlikely location, and you're not sure you are there until you see the Santa Claus over the door. As you walk inside, you'll notice there are Santa Claus figures everywhere--year round! As a matter of fact, little has changed over the past 30-plus years that the restaurant has been in operation. The steaks, pork chops, pasta, seafood and sandwiches are all excellent, but the unusual items on the menu are the Arabian dishes. The Arabian salad in a delicately light lemon dressing arrives in a bowl and is then folded into Arabian bread. Eggplant, stuffed cabbage leaves, and baked chicken Djage are also wonderful. A truly unique dining experience.

188. LORENZO'S BISTRO & BAKERY
972 South Hebron
Evansville, IN 47714
(812) 475-9477
Open Monday-Saturday for lunch & dinner. Closed Sunday.
Credit cards accepted.

Originally the Real Bread Company in downtown Evansville, Lorenzo's moved to its current location on the east side and brought its bakery along. European artisan breads are baked from scratch daily. There's also a bistro where lunch and dinner are served in an intimate European restaurant setting, decorated with awnings and umbrellas both inside and out. Daily lunch specials include soup, the popular quiche, crab melt, and interesting wraps, plus salads, sandwiches (hot brown or pastrami), and pasta dishes. Dinners feature seasonal entrees and appetizers that include unique presentations of hand-cut steaks, fresh seafood like ahi tuna, halibut and salmon, along with poultry, lamb and vegetarian selections. Dessert is always the perfect complement to a Lorenzo meal. Each day, the pastry chef prepares a variety of desserts such as the signature bread pudding, fresh strawberry cake, creme bruleé, French country carrot cake and a variety of cheesecakes.

189. RAFFI'S
1100 North Burkhardt
Evansville, IN 47715
(812) 479-9166
Open Monday-Saturday for dinner. Closed Sunday.
Credit cards accepted.

Raffi's has been offering casual fine dining since 1989, complete with white table-cloths, crystal, and candlelight. There is a classic bar, outdoor dining, and live jazz on selected nights. The specialties of the house feature a variety of delightful sauces made with herbs, wine and special ingredients served over pasta with your choice of chicken, veal, shrimp or fish. Traditional pasta and seafood entrees are also on the menu, along with rack of lamb, beef tenderloin and a Mediterranean style rib-eye steak for the red meat eaters! Whatever you choose, you will be pleased. A banquet room is available for private parties.

190. SHYLER'S BAR-B-Q GRILL
405 South Green River Road
Evansville, IN 47715
(812) 476-4599
Open daily for lunch & dinner.
Credit cards accepted.

Although the huge "General Store" sign suggests "est. 1991," you feel as if it's the '50's when you enter this establishment. James Dean and others are staring at you from the wall, "Wake Up Little Susie" is playing, and there are old Coca-Cola coolers in the aisles. Gasoline company logos decorate the light fixtures over the tables and gas pumps are lined up against the wall. Pictures of old cars should not surprise you when you find out that the restaurant was built on what was previously a used car lot! The owner learned about barbecue in Tennessee and has some tasty entrees to share with you. The pulled pork is delicious and comes with pickled onions on the plate. In addition to the Bar-B-Q, maple mustard or apple-glazed pork chop choices, there are ribs, chicken, sausage, burgers and sandwiches. All dinners are served with two homemade sides, and pies are made fresh daily. A roll of paper towels is on every table for those who look good in everything they eat!

191. BEECHWOOD INN
State Road 56
(1/2 mile north of French Lick Springs Resort)
French Lick, IN 46432
(812) 936-9012
Open Monday-Saturday for dinner. Closed Sunday.
Credit cards accepted.

The Inn is located in the 1915 home built by Charles Ballard, known in the past as owner of nightclubs, casinos, traveling circuses and the West Baden Springs Hotel. There is an obvious commitment and dedication to quality. All of the sauces start from homemade stock, and the butchering is done on site. Steaks and seafood are the most popular choices, and there is a variety of homemade desserts. Should you want to spend the night, six unique guest rooms, furnished with beautiful antiques, are available.

192. CHATEAU POMIJE
25060 Jacobs Road
Guilford, IN 47022
(800) 791-9463
Open Wednesday-Sunday for dinner; Sunday for lunch. Closed Monday & Tuesday.
Credit cards accepted.

Chateau Pomije is nestled on 100 acres amid some of Indiana's most picturesque scenery. It combines the captivating atmosphere of a fully working winery with the charm, elegance and character of the restaurant itself—a reconstructed 100-year-old timbered barn featuring a dramatic stone fireplace, the largest of its kind in Indiana. Begin with a tour of the winery and sample some of its award-winning wines. Then, sit down to a wonderful selection of homemade favorites: generous cuts of mouth-watering steak aged to perfection, delicious pork tenderloin, and Indiana's famous BBQ ribs and chicken, served with plenty of fresh vegetables, homegrown salads and bread. No one leaves hungry!

193. HAUB'S STEAK HOUSE
Corner of Main & Haub
Haubstadt, IN 47639
(812) 768-6462; (800) 654-1158
Open Monday-Saturday for dinner. Closed Sunday.
Credit cards accepted.

This former warehouse built in the early 1900's has been remodeled into a charming southern colonial straight out of Williamsburg. Decorated with wood paneling and large chandeliers, each dining room carries out the colonial theme. You can choose to dine in the Manor Room or the Kensington Room. There are over 50 entrees on the menu, including prime beef and fresh seafood. Reservations are recommended on weekends.

194. LOG INN

Off I-64 on Warrenton Road
Haubstadt, IN 47639
(812) 867-3216
Open Tuesday-Saturday for dinner.
Closed Sunday & Monday.
Cash or checks accepted.

Built in 1825 as one of the main noon day stage coach stops and trading posts between Evansville and Vincennes, this historic building is officially recognized as the oldest restaurant in Indiana and the oldest original log inn. The full cellar beneath the inn was also an underground railroad stop during the Civil War. Surrounded by many antiques, including the main bar, back bar and cash register purchased in 1892, and an old 1910 nickelodeon, you can dine on their specialty of fried chicken and family style dinners. Ask to be seated in the same original log room that Abraham Lincoln visited in November 1844!

195. NISBET INN

6701 Nisbet Road (I-64, Exit 18)
Haubstadt, IN 47639
(812) 963-9305
Open Tuesday-Saturday for lunch & dinner; Sundays on occasion. Closed Monday.
Credit cards accepted.

Located at the site of an old railroad crossing about 10 miles north of Evansville, the Inn was built in 1912 as an oasis for food, drink and lodging for the rail traveler. Even though a train hasn't passed through since 1971, the architecture has remained true to its original design, and it is still a popular place for food and drink. You will enjoy an atmosphere of warmth and hospitality where you can easily imagine yourself in an earlier and more relaxed time. Its reputation draws patrons from all over to sample some of the best barbecue around, along with a variety of sandwiches, homemade soups and pies. A nice selection of beer, wine and cocktails is available.

196. SCHNITZELBANK RESTAURANT

393 Third Avenue
Jasper, IN 47546
(812) 482-2640
Open Monday-Saturday for breakfast,
lunch & dinner. Closed Sunday.
Credit cards accepted.

This large, alpine-looking German restaurant, complete with a working Glockenspiel out front, is located on the original site of a small local tavern called Schnitzelbank, the name of a bench that woodcrafters whittle on. Outstanding German food is served by waitresses dressed in drindl skirts. The colorful murals on the walls of the dining rooms will transport you to the mountains of Germany! Wiener schnitzel and beef rolladen are house favorites, but steak, prime rib and hand-breaded shrimp are also available. The salad bar features 50 different items, including ribble (round German noodles) and turnip kraut. Sample one of the 100 different imported beers or order your favorite American brand.

197. SCHIMPFF'S CONFECTIONERY, LLC

347 Spring Street
Jeffersonville, IN 47130
(812) 283-8367
Open Monday-Saturday for lunch. Closed Sunday.
Credit cards accepted.

It is no surprise that Schimpff's has been designated as one of Indiana's "Hidden Treasures." The largest collection of brass drop rolls is on display here. What is a brass drop roll? Find out as you watch candy being made by the fourth generation owners. Ask questions and see the wonderful collection of candy memorabilia. Red hots are Schimpff's oldest continuously made candy, but they are also well-known for candy fish and horehound drops. Another favorite is the hand-dipped Modjeska, a caramel-covered marshmallow treat named after a famous Polish-born actress who performed in Ibsen's "A Doll's House" in 1883. After visiting the museum, grab a bite to eat at the lunch counter. In addition to the old standbys, you may want to try the Benedictine cheese sandwich. It is named after Jennie Benedict who owned a boarding house in the 1800's and served this sandwich of ground cucumber and cream cheese. There's also a soda fountain menu with shakes, root beer floats and sundaes.

198. WALL STREET CAFE

402 Wall Street
Jeffersonville, IN 47130
(812) 288-6466
Open Monday-Saturday for breakfast & lunch. Closed Sunday.
Cash only establishment.

Don't expect a restaurant where stockbrokers come to eat! This Wall Street cafe is a comfortable, family-operated establishment owned by a butcher who knows how to "hand pat" his own burgers. As a matter of fact, these burgers have been voted the best in Clark County! It is also reported that this is the only restaurant in the state that processes, bakes and hand-slices its own country ham. Thus, country ham and eggs is a favorite for breakfast. Phony eggs and "low fat, high taste" pork chops are also an option. Of course, hamburgers are at the top of the lunch menu, but one of the specials, like country ham and greens, may sound better to you.

199. WHISKY'S

334 Front Street
Lawrenceburg, IN 47025
(812) 537-4239
Open Monday-Friday for lunch & dinner; Saturday for dinner. Closed Sunday.
Credit cards accepted.

Old Lawrenceburg is the home of Seagram's Distillery, and the restaurant is named for its location in the "whiskey city!" Two buildings, one dating from 1850 and the other rumored to have been a button factory in 1835, are joined by an atrium and feature five dining areas: a formal dining room, the enclosed courtyard, the Malt Room, the Seagram's Room with a huge metal cut-out of a Seagram's bottle on the ceiling, and the cozy backroom bar. The overall atmosphere is dark and quiet with candles and fresh flowers on the tables. The atrium is decorated with a collection of birdhouses, and a post office from an old grocery store provides unique seating for four. Most in demand are the barbecued ribs, smoked with a secret sauce, but the steaks and house-smoked chicken are other popular selections.

200. THE OVERLOOK

1153 West State Road 62
(3 Miles South of I-64, Exit 92)
Leavenworth, IN 47137
(812) 739-4264
Open daily for breakfast, lunch & dinner.
Credit cards accepted.

Overlooking a sweeping panorama of forested hills and the Ohio River as it arches around a horseshoe bend, you will enjoy magnificent views from every window in this appropriately-named restaurant. The Overlook has earned a reputation over the years for good home cooking at very reasonable prices, offered in a warm and casual setting. Specialties include the popular creamed chicken served over homemade biscuits and a terrific beef manhattan. Steak, country fried chicken, ham, pork chops and seafood are additional selections. A nice variety of sandwiches is also available.

201. OLD BANK & CO.

59 South Main Street
Linton, IN 47441
(812) 847-3960
Open Tuesday-Friday for lunch & dinner; Saturday for dinner.
Closed Sunday & Monday.
Credit cards accepted.

An occasional passerby will walk into the old Peoples Trust Company, thinking the bank is still there! Bank offices have been converted into small glass-partitioned dining areas. Enjoy your meal in the Loan Department complete with money bags, the Accounting Department decorated with old calculators, the Millionaires Room accented with old checks, or the President's Office. The old bank vault with a 10,000 pound door now accommodates the wine cellar. A trip to the bathroom to view the decor is an extra treat! Featured specials are available at lunch. The menu includes various pasta dishes (carbonera, verona, chicken almondine) along with veal, steak and chicken items. The bar is constructed from the wood of an old teller's booth and provides a pleasant meeting place for visitors. Banquet facilities are available.

202. STOLL'S COUNTRY INN

State Road 54 West
Linton, IN 47441
(812) 847-2477
Open Monday-Saturday for breakfast, lunch & dinner; Sunday for lunch.
Credit cards accepted.

Enjoy country dining with an Amish influence in both the decor and the cooking. Everything is made from scratch and you can order off the menu or feast on the lunch or dinner buffet. Items on the buffet change daily, but might include the signature meatloaf, popular country fried chicken, steak, smoked sausage and kraut, plus real mashed potatoes and homemade noodles. There's even a "fix your own" ice cream sundae bar on the buffet. No alcohol is served. Catering is available.

203. KEY WEST SHRIMP HOUSE
117 Ferry Street
Madison, IN 47250
(812) 265-2831
Open Tuesday-Saturday for lunch & dinner.
Dinner menu all day Sunday. Closed Monday.
Credit cards accepted.

Dine in an old button factory while overlooking the Ohio River! This small family-owned restaurant has been serving customers here for over 30 years. Shrimp is the specialty: coconut, panama or fried. Frog legs, catfish, steak and chicken are also offered. The double-baked potato is good, and the extra thin garlic toast is unique. If you are in the area, the Shrimp House is a good place to eat and imagine what life was like in a town along the river.

204. MILAN RAILROAD INN
Main & Carr Streets
Milan, IN 47031
(812) 654-2800; (800) 448-7405
Open Tuesday-Sunday for lunch & dinner. Closed Monday.
Credit cards accepted.

Built in 1915 as the Keonig Hotel, the restaurant is situated next to the railroad tracks and at least six to eight trains pass through every day! For avid train fans, a front porch with three booths provides an excellent viewing area while enjoying your meal. Along with train memorabilia and old tools, the restaurant is also decorated with information about the town's memorable 1954 state championship basketball team featured in the movie "Hoosiers." The unique soup and salad bar features 18 different dishes including bread pudding with rum sauce, and "everything is homemade except the cottage cheese." The chef's seasonal specialties feature entrees such as pork Wellington in puff pastry, sesame-crusted salmon, and grilled pheasant breast with blueberry sage sauce. The more traditional items include the popular fried chicken, apple smoked pork chops, steaks, and Angus prime rib.

205. BONAPARTE'S RETREAT
8961 North US Highway 421
Napoleon, IN 47037
(812) 852-4343
Open Thursday-Sunday for lunch & dinner;
Wednesday for dinner. Closed Monday & Tuesday.
Credit cards accepted.

There's a wonderful secret in the small Indiana town of Napoleon: a restaurant originally built in 1830 that served as an Underground Railroad stop and now houses a collection of memorabilia about military genius Napoleon Bonaparte. The tables are decorated with fresh flowers from the local shop across the street, and a circular wooden bar welcomes the curious traveler. There are multiple choices of appetizers, soups, salads, sandwiches and hoagies. Specialty sandwiches carry historical names like the Bonaparte, the Napoleon, the Waterloo, and the Railroad House. Dinner entrees feature chicken, steak, fish and barbecued ribs, the house specialty. While in Napoleon, see if you can locate the Howard White life-size woodcarving of Napoleon Bonaparte!

206. NASHVILLE HOUSE

Main & VanBuren Streets
Nashville, IN 47448
(812) 988-4554
Open Wednesday-Monday for lunch
& dinner. Closed Tuesdays.
Credit cards accepted.

An Indiana restaurant guide would not be complete without mentioning the Nashville House, famous for its fried biscuits with homemade apple butter! Originally the site of a hotel built in 1859, that structure burned down in 1944 and was rebuilt in 1947 as a restaurant and country store. Native Brown County poplar and oak timbers and floors, red and white checked tablecloths, and a wonderful collection of antiques decorate the interior. In fact, the owner has been approached to sell his antiques, but he refuses, saying he wouldn't have anything to hang on the walls! Lunch features sandwiches served on wonderful homemade bread and daily specials, such as fried chicken livers and chicken salad made with yogurt and a little fruit for flavor—delicious! Country fried chicken, ham and turkey dinners are available all day. Special homemade desserts include the famous pecan nut pie, cobblers and cream pies.

207. RED GERANIUM

504 North Street
New Harmony, IN 47631
(812) 682-4431
Open daily for breakfast, lunch & dinner.
Credit cards accepted.

Established in 1964, the Red Geranium is one of the region's most charming and romantic restaurants. Serving breakfast, lunch and dinner seven days a week, the "Red" offers seasonal American cuisine and midwest favorites, along with an extensive choice of wines to accompany your meal. Diners may choose one of three distinctively different dining rooms. The Main Dining Room captures the romance and Old World charm of the nineteenth century. The Green Room offers comfortable benches and a cozy, casual atmosphere. Ornate hand-carved doors grace the entrance to the third room, the Tillich Room (named for philosopher Paul Tillich) and offers a panoramic, pastoral view of a serene lake. At night, the warmth of a large fireplace adds to the romantic setting of this room. The Grapevine Bar serves fine liquors, draft beers, and wines by the glass.

208. THE BRAU HAUS

22170 Wasser Strasse Street
Oldenburg, IN 47036
(812) 934-4840
Open Tuesday-Sunday for lunch & dinner.
Closed Monday.
Credit cards accepted.

Listed on the National Register of Historic Places, the town of Oldenburg is also known as the "Village of Spires," a vivid example of the old world German heritage in America. The restaurant's menu is filled with many traditional lunch and dinner items, such as homemade soups, sandwiches, steaks and seafood, but the specialties are the Brau Haus chicken and Oldenburg's Favorites: the Brau Haus reuben; home-made sausage pattie dinner; and fresh bratwurst with sauerkraut on rye. If you are in the area, you might enjoy combining a stop at The Brau Haus with a tour of this historic village.

209. JEEVES & COMPANY
64 South Main Street
Scottsburg, IN 47170
(812) 752-6559
Open daily for lunch & dinner.
Credit cards accepted.

The restaurant opened its doors on the town square in 1985 and the emphasis has always been to provide quality food and service in a relaxed atmosphere. The lunch menu offers a variety of soups, salads and sandwiches, while the dinner menu includes certified Angus steaks, chicken, seafood, pork and pasta dishes. Full bar service is available. There are forty different coffees and teas available in the gift shop, as well as a varied selection of pottery, glassware, kitchen items, jams, jellies, chocolates, candies and more.

210. CHICKEN HOUSE
7180 State Road 111
Sellersburg, IN 47172
(812) 246-9485
Open Monday-Friday for lunch & dinner;
Saturday for dinner. Closed Sunday.
Credit cards accepted.

As you drive along State Road 111 through the farmland of southern Indiana, you will come upon an old white house near the road with a sign saying "Restaurant." The local clientele in this "no frills" establishment say the house has been there for over 100 years, and most of the tables were reserved on a Saturday evening. People come for the fried chicken, but livers, gizzards, pan-fried oysters, and country ham are also available. The menu states that the food is prepared to order so it takes a little longer, but they pledge that "it is worth the extra time you wait."

211. CAFE at BATAR
12649 Highway 50 East
Seymour, IN 47274
(812) 522-8617
Open Thursday-Saturday for lunch. (Closed mid-December; re-opens April 1st.)
Credit cards accepted.

Pull off the highway, park your car, and as you open the door to step outside, take a deep breath--the scent will make you feel like you are surrounded by a pine forest! As a matter of fact, you are right next to the Muscatatuck National Wildlife Refuge. Sitting amidst the natural beauty is Cafe Batar, the Parlor Music Museum, and the Batar gift shop. Lunch is served in this quaint cafe that is filled with windows overlooking the colorful gardens visited by hummingbirds and butterflies. Antique wedgewood blue and white china is used to serve sandwiches, soups, salads and wraps, along with the weekly specials. Of course, the emphasis is on dessert with cherry cobbler and raspberry curl cake among the popular choices, but Bun-Apple Tite is the house specialty. After lunch, take some time to wander the garden, peruse the specialty items in the gift shop, and visit the museum with its collection of antique parlor music instruments and a "Life" magazine collection spanning 64 years.

212. CHOCOLATE SPOON
104 Chestnut Street
Seymour, IN 47274
(812) 524-8458
Open Monday-Friday for brunch & lunch. Special parties
and dinner by reservation (evenings and Saturdays).
Closed Sunday. Call to confirm hours.
Credit cards accepted.

If old buildings in downtown Seymour could tell their history, this one would say that, over the years, it has housed the first Seymour National Bank, McDonald & Appel (the Everything Place), and the Ritz Café. Now, as the Chocolate Spoon, it features a candy and sweet shop and a gourmet coffee bistro. It is a delightful spot to enjoy brunch, lunch or dinner. The menu includes fresh soups, salads, sandwiches and souffles, all served with homemade breads. Eva, the owner, takes great pride in the candies, pastries and desserts created in her kitchen. This is also a great place to arrange for catering the special events in your business or social life.

213. HILLTOP RESTAURANT
State Road 67 (north of Spencer)
Spencer, IN 47460
(812) 829-3891; (800) 504-4455
Open Wednesday-Saturday for dinner; Sunday for lunch & dinner.
Closed Monday & Tuesday.
Credit cards accepted.

Situated on a hilltop in Southern Indiana's "Sweet Owen" County, this restaurant has been a popular dining spot for over 50 years. Originally known as the Skyland Lodge, it boasted the reputation for fine family dining, a tradition it continues to uphold today. The atmosphere is casual and inviting with the words over the fireplace telling the story: "Thru our doors come the finest people in the land, our friends, you folk." The specialties are Spencer steak and fried chicken, which are accompanied by a feast: lettuce salad, tomato juice, pickled beets, vegetable sticks, mashed potatoes, gravy, green beans, corn and homemade rolls with orange marmalade. And if that isn't enough--treat yourself to Mississippi Mud Cake or persimmon pudding for dessert. Definitely the place to go with a hearty appetite!

214. JOE HUBER'S FAMILY FARM, ORCHARD & RESTAURANT

2421 Scottsville Road
Starlight, IN 47106
(812) 923-5255
Open daily for lunch & dinner. Closed December 24 through January 1.
Credit cards accepted.

Started in 1967 as a roadside fruit and vegetable market, it soon became a place where you could pick your own produce. The regular customers often commented that they would like something to eat, so in 1983, a restaurant was built adjacent to the market. Now seating 400, you are greeted by family portraits and a huge painting of the Huber farm covering one wall. You can also dine outdoors on the awning-covered patio, surrounded by beautiful flower, fruit and vegetable gardens. Seasonal produce from the Huber and surrounding farms accompany the main course selections of country-fried chicken or Huber honey ham. Homemade dumplings and deep fried biscuits are also tasty additions. Tempting desserts include fresh strawberry pie (in season), homemade peach cobbler and coconut or peanut butter cream pies. It is a smoke-free environment.

215. STORY INN

6404 South State Road 135
Story, IN 47448
(812) 988-2273
Open Tuesday-Sunday for breakfast,
lunch & dinner. Closed Monday.
Reservations requested for dinner.
Credit cards accepted.

Located in a village representative of a rural turn-of-the-century trading community, this charming country inn is a fun retreat for dinner after a day in Brown County or an athletic event at I.U. The main floor of this 1850's General Store is virtually unaltered and houses the gourmet restaurant. The menu features cuisine that is prepared in-house from fresh, seasonal ingredients, along with award-winning desserts and appetizers. Bed and Breakfast rooms are available upstairs and in surrounding cottages. The ultimate Story experience is dining on the screened porch during a heavy rain and hearing the raindrops fall on the tin roof!

216. PORT HOLE INN
8939 East South Shore Drive
Lake Lemon (south shore)
Unionville, IN 47468
(812) 339-1856
Open daily for lunch & dinner.
Credit cards accepted.

This little country tavern sits right off the road, making it an easy stop for people who are in the area and have a taste for juicy catfish, a steak, or perhaps just a sandwich. Popular side dishes to enjoy with the meal include hush puppies, potato cakes and slaw. You can eat in the bar or in the family dining area. Enjoy music on the weekends in season.

217. BLACK BUGGY
Highway 57
Washington, IN 47501
(812) 254-8966
Open Monday-Saturday for breakfast, lunch & dinner.
Closed Sunday.
Credit cards accepted.

As you approach the restaurant, you know you are at the right place when you see the black buggy on the roof and a buggy seat on the wall at the entrance announcing an opening date in 1996. The food is served buffet-style with entrees, salads, vegetables and desserts available at different stations. Food is plentiful but a sign cautions the customer to "Waste not, want not." The waitresses are dressed like the Amish, and the furnishings depict Amish life with quilts, dolls and signs decorating the interior. There are daily food and patron specials, plus a seafood buffet on Friday evenings.

218. CAFE AT SINCLAIR'S
West Baden Springs Hotel
8538 West Baden Avenue
West Baden Springs, IN 47469
(812) 936-9300
Open daily for breakfast & lunch; dinner by reservation only.
Credit cards accepted.

Once considered the Eighth Wonder of the World, the West Baden Springs Hotel has been restored to its former glorious state. Seeing the domed atrium (reportedly the world's largest dome) is a treat in itself. The attention to detail in the renovation of the hotel is absolutely remarkable. Sinclair's, named for the person who had the hotel built, is furnished with the same care. The overall look is formal with white tablecloths, dark woodwork, classic furniture and an abundance of glass. If you've never seen a purse stool, you will when you visit the restaurant! For lunch, you can have a salad, sandwich, panini or a main course of slow roasted range chicken or lemon parsley crusted salmon. There is also a Bar Pie, crisp pizza prepared in the woodstone brick oven. Antipasti, Zuppa and/or Insalata begin the evening meal, followed by the first course, usually a pasta dish like Gnocchi Balsamella. Secondi Piatti selections (main course) are from the fish or meat entrees: perhaps Apigola al Forno (sea bass) or Osso Buco (veal shank). No matter what you choose, eating in this fairy-tale hotel "castle" will be an extraordinary experience.

219. FRONT PORCH STEAK HOUSE
118 North Canal Street
Worthington, IN 47471
(812) 875-2306
Open Sunday & Tuesday for breakfast & lunch;
Wednesday-Saturday for breakfast, lunch & dinner. Closed Monday.
Cash or checks accepted.

Originally an old filling station, much has been done to create a warm and inviting atmosphere in this restaurant, specializing in wonderful home cooked meals and homemade pies. The interior was divided into sections for dining areas, cathedral ceilings added, and accent shelves installed to display a collection of crockery and antiques. The Rose Room with its carpeted walls is a nice addition. Benches on the front porch invite you to sit and relax before or after your meal. They are well known for excellent steaks, catfish, and spaghetti with homemade sauce, but people come from all over for the prime rib on Friday and Saturday and the popular pan-fried chicken on Sunday. There is also a variety of lunch specials, featuring items such as pinto beans and Alaskan pollack, and the traditional breakfast fare.

BORDER STATES

Michigan

220. TABOR HILL WINERY RESTAURANT
185 Mt. Tabor Road
Buchanan, MI 49107
(800) 283-3363
Open Wednesday-Sunday for lunch & dinner.
Closed Monday & Tuesday.
Credit cards accepted.

Tabor Hill Winery is on the Southwest Michigan Wine Trail and has been producing wines for almost 40 years. After driving through the rolling countryside to the restaurant, you are welcomed by the sign, "Drink wine, laugh often, live long." You can dine overlooking the vineyards and enjoy a meal accompanied by the perfect wine. Kahlua ham on a croissant and baked seafood focaccia are sandwiches offered for lunch, in addition to the salads and special entrees such as tilapia, tuna, crab cakes, and raspberry chicken. The dinner menu changes daily and has multiple starters for you to taste as you sip your wine. Halibut, scallops, duck and bison "osso bucco" are possible main course choices. There's also a vegetarian lasagna with portobello mushrooms, eggplant and tofu. Wine tasting and wine shopping are also available at the restaurant.

221. HANNAH'S
115 South Whittaker
New Buffalo, MI 49117
(888) 877-1440
Open daily for lunch & dinner.
Credit cards accepted.

Hannah's is located just across the Indiana/Michigan border (I-94, Exit #1) in the quaint town of New Buffalo where you will find a variety of wonderful shops and unique boutiques. When you need a break from a day of shopping, this is the perfect place to stop for lunch or dinner. Formerly a house built in 1895, the owners have created a warm and friendly atmosphere and their genuine hospitality makes you feel like a guest in their home. The decor is an eclectic collection of antiques and artifacts, and pictures of friends and family from years past decorate the walls. The menu is one of the most extensive in the area, catering to everyone's tastes and featuring a nice selection of appetizers, entrees, sandwiches, salads and vegetarian dishes. The full roasted prime rib and Bohemian roast duck and pork, served with dumplings and sauerkraut, are popular dinner choices.

222. O'BRIENS RESTAURANT & BAR
Whittaker Woods Golf Community
12578 Wilson Road
New Buffalo, MI 49117
(269) 469-3400
Open daily for lunch & dinner.
Credit cards accepted.

Just across the Indiana border, right off I-94, you will find a golf course in a secluded place with scenic fairways set in the natural wetlands of the area. Whether you are looking for a casual meal or a more formal one, O'Briens has a dining venue to suit you. In good weather, you can choose to eat on the deck. If dining inside, an abundance of windows brings the beautiful outdoors to your table. Some highlights from the extensive menu include O'Brien chips, sweet and sour cabbage soup, Whittaker salad, calamari fritta, O'Brien burger, buffalo chicken wrap, fisherman's pasta, and liver and onions. You don't have to play golf to enjoy eating at O'Briens!

223. REDAMAK'S
616 East Buffalo Street
New Buffalo, MI 49117
(269) 469-4522
Open daily for lunch & dinner. (March 1-end of October)
Cash only establishment.

For over thirty years, Redamak's has been famous throughout the area for fresh, hearty, juicy burgers. People travel from miles around to "Bite Into A Legend!" Each burger is prepared fresh and then dressed to your liking. Every bite is mouth-watering and juicy! Designed with the whole family in mind, the menu also offers a wide variety of delicious sandwiches, dinners, finger foods and kids' choices, along with a nice selection of soft drinks, bottle and draft beers, wine, and cocktails to complement your meal. A newly renovated three season room is a great place for family gatherings, special events, and business meetings.

224. THORNTON'S HOME TOWN CAFE
613 Pleasant Street
St. Joseph, MI 49085
(269) 983-0932
Open daily for breakfast & lunch.
Credit cards accepted.

Located in this resort town on the shore of Lake Michigan, Thornton's is a great place to stop and enjoy real home town cooking. Jumbo omelettes are featured and there's a Wall of Fame for those who eat all of "Bob's Big Bomb," an omelette filled with corned beef hash, bacon, sausage, ham, mushrooms, green peppers, onion, tomato, American, Swiss, and cheddar cheese! The "Hand Grenade" is a smaller version of the big bomb. Traditional omelettes, pancakes, French toast, waffles and biscuits and gravy are acceptable and tasty alternatives. Besides the daily lunch specials, there are multiple choices of hot and cold sandwiches, soup and salad plates, seafood, and the house favorites of chicken or tuna wraps, super nachos and quesadillas. You will appreciate the cafe's home town atmosphere, complete with blue and white checked tablecloths, and the home town service to go with it!

225. FROEHLICH'S
26 North Elm Street
Three Oaks, MI 49128
(866) 626-5267
Call ahead for seasonal hours.
Credit cards accepted.

Combine shopping with tasting as you browse the shelves and display cases at Froehlich's. "Made from scratch" breads like honey sunflower, cinnamon, peasant, and herb cheese are made on the premises daily, along with muffins, bagels and wonderful crackers. A variety of products are "put up" in jars with jams and preserves being the most plentiful. You'll also enjoy looking at all the housewares and furnishings on the shelves, including a wide variety of one-of-a-kind gift items. Eventually, you make your way to the counter where you can order fresh homemade sandwiches, soups, salads and cookies! Several tables invite you to eat inside, but a table outside is a delightful place to sip a cup of coffee, eat a muffin and enjoy.

Ohio

226. JEFF RUBY'S
700 Walnut Street
Cincinnati, OH
(513) 784-1200
Open Monday-Saturday for dinner. Closed Sunday.
Credit cards accepted.

Dress up in your finest attire and head to Jeff Ruby's for a memorable dining experience. This is a classy, 1940's New York-style steakhouse with "machismo," complete with piano bar and a wine cellar that not only stores 140 different red wines, but also serves as a private dining room. You are introduced to the Art Deco-themed interior in the hotel-style lobby where you can relax and enjoy a cocktail by the fireplace before heading to the luxurious dining room. High quality, succulent steaks are the specialty, dry-aged in an exhibition room that is visible from the street. The rest of the menu offers a broad selection of appetizers, notably the jumbo cocktail shrimp and pan-fried crabcakes, signature salads, and potato dishes to accompany your entree. The portions are large and extravagant, and the service and atmosphere are incomparable. Enjoy live jazz performances on Mondays, Tuesdays, and Thursdays.

227. JEAN-ROBERT at PIGALL'S
127 West Fourth Street
Cincinnati, OH 45202
(513) 721-1345
Open Tuesday-Saturday for dinner. Closed Sunday & Monday.
Credit cards accepted.

The chef and his creations are the reason to dine at Pigall's, but the pristine environment which exudes excellence adds extra joy to the dining experience. Many years ago, this building, located in a national historic neighborhood, housed the original five-star restaurant called Pigall's. Jean-Robert nurtured his culinary skills in Europe, the British West Indies, and New York City, and eventually brought his contemporary French cuisine to Cincinnati. In 2002, he honored a memory by joining his name to that of the Pigall's of the past. An innovative three or five course prix-fixe seasonal menu offers a wide selection of hors d'oeuvres, entrees and desserts. Each item is deliciously explained in the menu, but you may want to use the expertise of the staff to design your meal. Jean-Robert has a table in the kitchen that you can reserve and watch the master at work. Pigall's has been said to present "the taste of Paris in the comfort of Cincinnati." Reservations are a must.

228. SCOTTI'S ITALIAN RESTAURANT
919 Vine Street
Cincinnati, OH 45202
(513) 721-9484
Open Tuesday-Saturday for lunch & dinner. Closed Sunday & Monday.
Credit cards accepted.

Established in 1912 and now fifth generation owned and operated, the restaurant is named after a close friend of the original owner, Salvatore Scoleri. The friend happened to be a famous Metropolitan Opera singer, Antonio Scotti. Strings of bottles hang across the ceiling and the walls are covered with ceramic tiles of various shapes and sizes. Burning candles provide the only light in the dining room, and there is soft music playing in the background. In addition to the beef, veal and chicken selections, there are various types of pasta dishes with about 15 different choices of sauces. Some pasta is homemade, and they cut their own steaks.

229. THE PRECINCT
311 Delta Avenue
Cincinnati, OH 45226
(513) 321-5454
Open daily for dinner.
Credit cards accepted.

Listed in the National Register of Historic Landmarks, this outstanding steakhouse was originally a police precinct station, located four miles from downtown. When first opened in 1981, the jail was part of the original decor, but today the brick walls are decorated with life-size photographs of the past. Frequented regularly by baseball players and other celebrities, there are colorful caricatures of these visitors hanging everywhere. All steaks are 28-day aged and considered to be the finest beef in America. Note the "Celebrity Steaks" on the menu with interesting combinations of sauces and seasonings.

230. TINKS CAFE

3410 Telford
Cincinnati, OH 45220
(513) 961-6500
Open Monday-Friday for lunch & dinner; Saturday & Sunday for dinner.
Credit cards accepted.

In the Gaslight District near the university, around the corner from the Esquire Theater, there is a restaurant that used to be the post office and now provides jazz music, a full-service bar, and a menu with imagination. In this comfortable spot with a neighborhood feeling, you may see people in suits or in jeans at lunchtime. In the evening, folks stop by for a drink and appetizers before attending the theater and/or for dinner and dessert after the show. Fried green tomatoes and mussels are favorite appetizers. Beef portobella bruschetta, seafood capellini, and wild mushroom penne are popular entrees. Tinks provides a non-smoking environment. By the way, Tinks was the name of the former owner's dog!

231. ZIP'S CAFE

1036 Delta Avenue
Cincinnati, OH 45208
(513) 871-9876
Open daily for lunch & dinner.
Credit cards accepted.

When Zip's opened in 1926, the cheeseburger cost 20 cents and peanut butter and jelly sandwiches cost 15 cents. The prices on the menu have changed, but the place maintains its original look with memorabilia of the past on the walls. A train travels above the booths passing a mural of the facades of the town buildings. People return to Zip's on Mt. Lookout Square, remembering the olden days and the Zip Burger on a Klosterman Bakery bun, which according to many was and still is the "best burger" in town. Zip's is also famous for its chili, which you can carry out by the half-gallon. The onion rings and cheese and/or chili fries are worth the splurge. The dessert choice changes daily.

232. BARRESI'S

4111 Webster Avenue
Deer Park, OH 45236
(513) 793-2540
Open Tuesday-Saturday for dinner. Closed Sunday & Monday.
Credit cards accepted.

This family-owned and honored establishment began as a small deli and has steadily increased in size, now considered one of the best Italian restaurants around. The owner's mother was from southern Italy; his father from the north. Thus, the menu offers a pleasant blend of flavors. Fresh flowers are on the tables, creating a comfortably elegant atmosphere. Traditional pasta dishes with multiple sauce choices are available, along with steaks, veal, chicken and seafood. The menu is extensive, but every entree is personally cooked and served "apiacere."

233. GRAND FINALE

3 East Sharon Avenue
Glendale, OH 45246
(513) 771-5925
Open Tuesday-Saturday for lunch & dinner;
Sunday for brunch & dinner. Closed Monday.
Credit cards accepted.

The Victorian landmark was originally an 1895 saloon with all the history that goes with it! Today, after 30 years of creative excellence by the original chef/owners, Grand Finale earns its award-winning reputation. The authentic antique decor is warm and charming with fresh flowers on every table. The candlelit awning-covered courtyard offers a year-round romantic ambiance. In the "Attic," an eclectic collection of art and memorabilia decorates the two private dining galleries. A creative menu features fine wines, fresh fish, superb steaks, lamb, veal, and the popular "Chicken Ginger." But the "Grand Finale" is the luscious homemade desserts that have made them famous!

234. GOLDEN LAMB

27 South Broadway
Lebanon, OH 45036
(513) 932-5065
Open daily for lunch & dinner.
Credit cards accepted.

Recognized as the oldest inn in Ohio, circa 1803, the Golden Lamb grew to become a nationally known hostelry and has played host to many prominent literary and political figures of the 19th century: Charles Dickens, Mark Twain, and twelve presidents, including Grant, John Quincy Adams, McKinley and Harding. The inn flourished during the days of coach travel, and many drivers and travelers, unable to read, were simply told to drive to "the sign of the golden lamb." Today, there are four public and five private dining rooms furnished in antiques of the period. The restaurant features traditional American fare and is served with the warmth and hospitality of a by-gone era. Diners are invited to explore the beautifully furnished hotel rooms named after famous guests. You can also view the fine collection of Shaker pieces and Currier and Ives prints on the upper floors.

Kentucky

235. ASIATIQUE RESTAURANT
1767 Bardstown Road
Louisville, KY 40205
(502) 451-2749
Open daily for dinner.
Credit cards accepted.

Bardstown Road is a busy place at mealtime. In contrast to other restaurants in the area, Asiatique is set off the street, up and down a few steps. The cuisine is considered "Pacific Rim," which means a fusion of the flavors and cooking techniques of East and West. Obviously, many cultures are involved in the creative recipes and the food offers a tasty alternative to the norm. Consider as starters: Vietnamese pork and shrimp with sweet chili-basil sauce, or scallops with fresh fruit chutney. Entrees include wok-seared Pacific salmon, ginger-crusted sea bass with noodle vegetables, and hoisin-marinated Pekin duck breast. To top off the meal, try a fresh grilled banana with ginger ice cream and a kahlua-chocolate drizzle. The already outstanding dining experience is enhanced by the attractive surroundings.

236. BAXTER STATION BAR & GRILL
1201 Payne Street
Louisville, KY 40204
(502) 584-1635
Open Monday-Saturday for lunch & dinner. Closed Sunday.
Credit cards accepted.

Once you step inside Baxter's, you are actually on a train! It's a long, narrow restaurant with overhead racks, scenes of the countryside through windows, and a train that travels a track around the ceiling. The board advertises the specials, and the menu features appetizers of fried green tomatoes, pan steamed mussels, and hummus Baxter. A Brutus salad with smoked bacon and spicy almonds, a black and bleu burger, or red beans and rice are enticing lunch choices. For dinner, there's ginger lime scallops, Payne Street ribs and salmon croquettes. Save room for the "made in-house" desserts--the key lime pie and derby pie are scrumptious! All aboard for good food!

237. JACK FRY'S
1007 Bardstown Road
Louisville, KY 40204
(502) 452-9244
Open Monday-Friday for lunch; every day for dinner.
Credit cards accepted.

Jack Fry and Flossie opened the restaurant at this location in 1933. Jack was a sports, horse racing and gambling enthusiast; thus, it became a sportsman's hangout with bookmaking in the back room! The decor changed when the restaurant was sold in 1972, but new owners in 1983 restored the original look from pictures that had been on the walls. The tin ceiling, white and black checked floor, and wooden booths with little lights are all features from the past. The food is as special as its history. Lunch choices feature Jack's Burger, shrimp wrap, or salmon and baby spinach salad. Dinner appetizers include shrimp and grits, scallops, and spicy fried oysters. Entrees are special preparations of veal, lamb, fish and even a vegetarian dish: potato gratin. To top off your meal, try the banana caramel pie, peach cobbler, or chocolate truffle torte.

238. LILLY'S CAFE & BISTRO

1147 Bardstown Road
Louisville, KY 40204
(502) 451-0447
Open Tuesday-Saturday for lunch & dinner.
Closed Sunday & Monday.
Credit cards accepted.

Brightly colored walls filled with an eclectic art collection add to the warm and welcoming atmosphere in this upscale neighborhood bistro. Chef/owner Kathy Cary says the cuisine has "no boundaries," meaning her ideas are always evolving around foods based on her Kentucky heritage and the American South, but continually influenced by her love of travel, both home and abroad. The menu is centered around seasonal, locally grown and raised produce and meats that are transformed into incredible entrees with inventive combinations of ingredients. For lunch, there's a roasted beet salad, slow roasted pork shoulder quesadilla filled with spinach, Capriole goat cheese, grilled onions and almond hazelnut mole, and an open-faced grilled eggplant, roasted pepper and fennel tampenade. Creative dinner entrees include veal scaloppini with crispy sweetbreads, rib pork chop and Newsom's ham stuffed Vidalia onion, duck two ways, and the "God Bless Our Local Farmers" plate, a wonderful combination of stuffed pepper, baby squash, cheddar cheese, baby green beans, and pickled mushrooms. Desserts abound, along with a nice selection of wines.

239. LIMESTONE RESTAURANT

10001 Forest Green Boulevard
Louisville, KY 40223
(502) 426-7477
Open Monday-Friday for lunch & dinner; Saturday for dinner; Sunday for brunch.
Credit cards accepted.

This casual, upscale restaurant is named primarily for the limestone contained in the Kentucky spring water that contributes to the development of both sour-mash bourbon whiskies and the thoroughbred race horses that drink the water. The goal of the chef/owners is to retain the charm of southern-style cooking for which the region is known while adding a contemporary twist to traditional dishes, using regional ingredients as much as possible. From Kentucky rainbow trout and freshwater shrimp to seared filet of Angus beef tenderloin and rack of lamb entrees, there is something for everyone on the dinner menu. Lunch features weekly specials, along with creative options of vegetarian pot pie, turkey crepes, and the popular Limestone reuben. If you can't decide what to order, ask for the "Feed Me, Chef," a five course spontaneous tasting menu available anytime for your entire table.

240. LYNN'S PARADISE CAFE

984 Barret Avenue
Louisville, KY 40204
(502) 583-3447
Open Monday for breakfast & lunch;
Tuesday-Sunday for breakfast, lunch & dinner.
Credit cards accepted.

"Eat and be happy" is the motto here and you'll be smiling before you enter the restaurant! A huge coffee pot pouring liquid into a cup is out front. Once inside, your senses are stimulated by a kaleidoscope of colors, "wacky" decor, and bustling activity. Mannequin legs in Lynn's Magic Pants decorate the windows; the staff is busily skewering peppers, olives and mushrooms for Bloody Marys at a Tiki bar; paper cut placemats, shell mobiles, and a thousand-plus tea bag "glob" hang from the ceiling; and a myriad of pictures fill the walls. The food is equally enjoyable. Breakfast specials that catch your attention are crunch cakes (with granola), pancakes made with cornmeal and wheat flour, a Popeye omelet, veggie biscuits and gravy, and BLT fried potatoes. Lunch adds a harvest moon chicken salad, Paradise hot brown, an entree of mom's meatloaf, or walnut-crusted chicken. Sides make the mouth water: cheese grits, roasted garlic mashed potatoes, herb braised lima beans, sage bread dressing, pan-fried apples, and sweet potato fries with cinnamon spice. Lynn's Paradise is quirky, fun and worth a trip to Louisville!

241. SEVICHE

1538 Bardstown Road
Louisville, KY 40205
(502) 473-8560
Open daily for dinner.
Credit cards accepted.

Described as one of the best and most innovative Nuevo Latino-style restaurants, the food served is a creative blend of flavors and traditions acquired through the chef/owner's Mexican and Puerto Rican heritage. The restaurant's name "Seviche" also describes the house specialties: a type of Latino sushi, although not quite raw. Fish or seafood is marinated in citrus juice, literally "cooking" in the sharply acidic marinade, losing its raw translucency and texture during the process. There are about a dozen seviches offered daily: rare sushi grade tuna with tomato vodka horseradish broth or with lemon-cilantro mojo sauce; an Italian version sashimi with lemon truffle mojo; or a Peruvian-Japanese style ceviche slices with rocoto chili and ginger mojo, to name just a few. Unique "Entradas" or entrees include pan roasted Florida snapper, beef tenderloin medallions topped with fried eggs, carmelized onions and chimichurri, and a famous Brazilian dish of black beans and various cuttings of meat served over rice with fresh salsa, braised greens and manioc flour. The creative menu, stylish decor and excellent service combine for a wonderful dining experience.

Things to Do and See
Along the Way...

ANDERSON
Historical Military Armor Museum
2330 Crystal Street
Anderson, IN 46012
(765) 649-8265

History awaits you with a hands-on experience of this collection of yesterday's and today's great war machines.

AUBURN
Auburn Cord Duesenberg Museum
1600 South Wayne Street
Auburn, IN 46706
(260) 925-1444

Listed in the National Registry of Historic Places, this 80,000 square-foot building houses over 100 fascinating antique and classic cars from the early 1900's.

BATTLE GROUND
Wolf Park
4004 East 800 North
Battle Ground, IN 47920
(765) 567-2265

Visitors can see wolves at close range living in a large naturalistic enclosure. Wolf Park is also home to foxes and a small herd of bison which are often included in the presentations.

BEDFORD
Blue Spring Cavern Caves
1459 Bluespring Caverns Road
Bedford, IN 47421
(812) 279-9471

Explore America's longest underground river by boat. Camp overnight in Canyon Hall, high above the hidden banks of Myst'ry River.

Turner Doll Factory
Off Hwy 58
Heltonville, IN 47436
(812) 834-6692

This is one of the few remaining handmade doll factories in the nation. Visit the factory to watch dolls being handcrafted from start to finish.

BRISTOW
Mary Rose Herb Farm & Retreat
23112 Cattail Road
Bristow, IN 47515
(812) 357-2699

A spiritual retreat, herbal and holistic health education center, and nature park where overnight guests can stay in unique tent-like abodes called "yurts."

CHESTERTON
Indiana Dunes Environmental Learning Center
700 Howe Road
Chesterton, IN 46304
(219) 395-9555

With the Indiana Dunes National Lakeshore as its classroom, students of all ages can learn about the relationship between people and the environment. Visit the dunes while you're there.

Yellow Brick Road Gift Shop & Oz Museum
109 East 950 North
Chesterton, IN 46304
(219) 926-7048

View Wizard of Oz memorabilia from this movie classic, most donated by cast members or their heirs. Gift shop filled with Oz collectibles.

Things to Do and See
Along the Way...

CLARKSVILLE
Falls of the Ohio State Park
201 West Riverside Drive
Clarksville, IN 47129
(812) 280-9970

The 386-million-year-old fossil beds in the park are among the largest naturally exposed Devonian fossil beds (coral reef) in the world.

COLUMBUS
Columbus Area Visitors Center
506 Fifth Street
Columbus, IN 47201
(812) 378-2622

The Columbus Area Visitors Center, a renovated home built in the early 1860's, is the starting point for a walking tour that showcases the city's fine architecture, public art, gardens and landscaping.

CORYDON
First State Capitol Building
200 North Capitol Avenue
Corydon, IN 47112
(812) 738-8241

Visitors can tour the original capitol building (cr. 1816) and Governor Hendricks's headquarters. The site also includes an informative visitors' center.

Zimmerman Art Glass Co.
395 Valley Road
Corydon, IN 47112
(812) 738-2206

This is a rare opportunity to see third-generation artists work in the time-honored method of individual glass sculpting as practiced by Colonial craftsmen.

CRAWFORDSVILLE
**General Lew Wallace Study
& Ben-Hur Museum**
200 Wallace Avenue
Crawfordsville, IN 47933
(765) 362-5769

Listed on the National Register of Historic Places, the museum is located within the private study of Major General Lew Wallace, the author of Ben-Hur. Items on display include memorabilia from his life as an author, soldier, statesman, artist, violinist and inventor.

DALE
Dr. Ted's Musical Marvels
11896 South US 231
Dale, IN 47523
(812) 937-4250

See this spectacular collection of the most amazing mechanical musical instruments you will ever hear from the 1800's to mid-1900's.

DANA
Ernie Pyle State Historic Site
120 Briarwood
Dana, IN 47847
(765) 665-3633

This historic site includes the house where World War II reporter Ernie Pyle was born and a state-of-the-art visitor center. Visitors will learn about this daring and respected Hoosier reporter.

Things to Do and See
Along the Way...

EVANSVILLE
Willard Library
21 First Avenue
Evansville, IN 47710
(812) 425-4309

Housed in a 110-year-old historic Victorian Gothic building, it is the oldest public library building in the state. Legend states it's a living, breathing haunted house!

FERDINAND
Monastery of the Immaculate Conception
802 East 10th Street
Ferdinand, IN 47532
(812) 367-1411

Listed in the National Register of Historic Places, you can take a tour of the church, grounds and architecturally magnificent monastery.

FISHERS
Conner Prairie
13400 Allisonville Road
Fishers, IN 46038
(317) 776-6000

A 1,400-acre nationally acclaimed living history museum where costumed interpreters depict the life and times of early settlers in an 1836 village. The grounds include a Visitors Center, picnic area, restaurant, and gift shop.

FORT WAYNE
Lincoln Museum
200 East Berry Street
Fort Wayne, IN 46802
(260) 455-3864

This award-winning exhibit features eleven galleries with hundreds of artifacts from Lincoln's era.

Allen County Public Library
Genealogy Research Department
900 Library Plaza
Fort Wayne, IN 46802
(260) 421-1200

Visit the largest public genealogy research library in America. Free services for both the beginning and advanced researchers.

GOSHEN
Old Bag Factory
1100 North Chicago Avenue
Goshen, IN 46528
(574) 534-2502

This historic 80,000 sq. ft. building, originally a bag factory, houses a gallery of specialty shops and artisan workshops.

HAGERSTOWN
Abbott's Candy Shop
48 East Walnut Street
Hagerstown, IN 47346
(765) 489-4442

The big pink and white building is a favorite stop for families who come to watch the candy-making process. Final stop on the tour is to see the chocolates being packed in their elegant gift boxes.

HOBART
Albanese Candy Factory
& Outlet Store
5441 East US 30
Hobart, IN 46410
(219) 947-3070

See gummies and chocolates being made, along with the world's tallest chocolate waterfall—an experience that children and adults won't soon forget!

Things to Do and See
Along the Way...

HUNTINGTON
Dan Quayle Center/United States Vice Presidential Museum
815 Warren Street
Huntington, IN 46750
(260) 356-6356

This is the only vice presidential museum in the world featuring artifacts from every U.S. vice president in history.

INDIANAPOLIS
Children's Museum of Indianapolis
3000 North Meridian Street
Indianapolis, IN 46208
(317) 334-3322

The largest children's museum in the world houses 11 major galleries that explore the physical and natural sciences, history, world cultures and the arts. Whenever possible, exhibits are "hands-on" or participatory in nature.

Crown Hill Cemetery
700 West 38th Street
Indianapolis, IN 46208
(317) 925-8231

One of the most historically significant sites in Indiana, Crown Hill is the burial site of many of Indiana's most famous people and public servants. The beautiful grounds include a large population of wildlife and over 150 species of trees and plant life.

The Eiteljorg Museum
500 West Washington Street
Indianapolis, IN 46204
(317) 636-WEST (9378)

The only museum of its kind in the Midwest, it contains one of the best Native American and Western art collections in the world.

Fort Harrison State Park
5753 Glenn Road
Indianapolis, IN 46216
(317) 591-0904

The park includes one of the largest tracts of hardwood forest in Central Indiana. Activities available include: cultural arts programs, a nature center, fishing, hiking and biking trails, saddle barn with horses, and the famous Fort Harrison Golf Course.

Indiana State Museum
650 W. Washington Street
Indianapolis, IN 46204
(317) 232-1637

With over 40,000 square feet of exhibit space and over 300,000 artifacts in collections, the museum covers the history of the natural world, Native Americans, cultural history, and the future of Indiana. It is the location of one of only four IMAX theaters in Indiana.

Speedway Hall of Fame Museum
4790 West 16th Street
Indianapolis, IN 46222
(317) 492-6784

Learn about the history of auto racing and view approximately 75 vehicles on display at all times. Bus tours of the historic 2.5-mile oval are available.

Indianapolis Museum of Art
4000 Michigan Road
Indianapolis, IN 46208
(317) 920-2651

The museum boasts a permanent historical collection of more than 50,000 works of art. Tour the Virginia B. Fairbanks Art and Nature Park and Oldfields-Lilly House and Gardens.

Things to Do and See
Along the Way...

Madame Walker Theatre Center
617 Indiana Avenue
Indianapolis, IN 46202
(317) 236-2099

Located in the restored 1920 headquarters of Madame C.J. Walker, the first self-made African-American female millionaire in the country, the Center is dedicated to celebrating arts and culture from an African-American perspective, along with events directed toward cross-cultural appreciation.

KENDALLVILLE
Mid America Windmill Museum
732 South Allen Chapel Road
Kendallville, IN 46755
(260) 347-2334

Learn about the evolution of wind power in the only known operational museum of its kind in the United States.

KNIGHTSTOWN
Hoosier Gymnasium
355 North Washington Street
Knightstown, IN 46148
(765) 345-2626; (317) 590-7854

This famous gym was home to the Hickory Huskers in "Hoosiers." Shoot a basket from where Jimmy made the game-winning shot or just sit in the stands and relive one of the greatest sports movies of all time. Call for times.

LINCOLN CITY
Lincoln Boyhood National Memorial
2916 East South Street
Lincoln City, IN 47552
(812) 937-4541

The first national park established in Indiana, it preserves the site of the farm where Abraham Lincoln lived during his formative years.

LOGANSPORT
Cass County Dentzel Carousel
Riverside Park
1212 Riverside Drive
Logansport, IN 46947
(574) 753-8725

Listed as a National Historic Landmark, this beautifully restored merry-go-round is a masterpiece of carving by Gustav Dentzel, tracing back to at least 1902. For only 50 cents, you can reach for the golden ring from your choice of 44 hand-carved animals and chariots.

MARENGO
Marengo Cave
400 East State Road 64
Marengo, IN 47140
(888) 702-2837

Take a leisurely tour through the Crystal Palace, pan for gemstones, twist and crawl through the cave simulator, or explore an undeveloped natural cave in this US National landmark.

MIDDLEBURY
Deutsch Kase House Cheese Factory
11275 County Road 250 North
Middlebury, IN 46540
(574) 825-9511

Watch skilled Amish cheese-makers turn local milk into award-winning cheese that is available to sample and take home.

NASHVILLE
Melchior Marionette Theatre
86 South Van Buren Street
Nashville, IN 47448
(800) 849-4853

This unique outdoor venue features a 20 minute family-oriented cabaret variety show with handcrafted marionettes. Call for performance schedule.

Things to Do and See
Along the Way...

T.C. Steele's State Historic Site
4220 T.C. Steele Road
Nashville, IN 47448
(812) 988-2785

Guided tours of the House of the Singing Winds, the studio where changing exhibits display Steele's work, are scheduled regularly. You can also visit the Dewar Log Cabin and the 90 acre Selma Steele Nature Preserve.

NEW CASTLE
Indiana Basketball Hall of Fame
One Hall of Fame Court
New Castle, IN 47362
(765) 529-1891

Located near the world's largest high school gym, the museum features numerous displays, exhibits, artifacts and memorabilia depicting Indiana high school basketball history. Visit the locker room for John Wooden's "pep talk!"

NEW HARMONY
Historic New Harmony
603 West Street
New Harmony, IN 47631
(812) 682-3816 (Museum Shop)

One of the most significant utopian communities in America, this is a place where three centuries of architecture, history and innovation interact.

PERU
Circus Hall of Fame
3076 East Circus Lane
Peru, IN 46970
(765) 472-7553

The museum's collection includes vintage circus wagons, steam calliopes, costumes of famous performers, circus props and other artifacts, posters, lithographs and handbills from circuses around the world.

Grissom Air Museum
1000 North Hoosier Boulevard
Peru, IN 46970
(765) 689-8011

One of the nation's fastest growing aviation museums, you can learn about historic aircraft, climb the Observation Tower, view exciting exhibits, and enjoy a modern, hands-on facility.

RISING SUN
Harps on Main
222 Main Street
Rising Sun, IN 47040
(812) 438-3032

See the harps being made, play any of them and peruse the selection of harp music, accessories and uncommon harp and Celtic gifts. Concerts every first Friday of the month.

ROCKVILLE
Billie Creek Village
1659 East US Highway 36
Rockville, IN 47872
(765) 569-5226

Indiana's only recreated, turn-of-the-century village and farmstead has a total of 38 authentic buildings and exhibits. Entertainment and educational opportunities are available year-round, from one of the country's best Civil War re-enactments to the Covered Bridge Festival.

SILVER LAKE
Whetstone Woodenware
110 East Main Street
Silver Lake, IN 46982
(260) 352-2093; (800) 253-3670

Stop in and see handcrafted kitchen tools being made from fine maple in this family-owned business.

Things to Do and See Along the Way...

SOUTH BEND
South Bend Chocolate Factory
3300 West Sample Street
South Bend, IN 46619
(574) 233-2577

Take a factory tour where you can sample straight off the production line and view one of the world's largest collections of chocolate-related artifacts.

STARLIGHT
The Forest Discovery Center
533 Louis Smith Road
Starlight, IN 47106
(812) 923-1590

Discover the wonders of the forest and the importance of trees at this interactive, educational facility with indoor forest, theater, activity area and workshop.

TERRE HAUTE
Clabber Girl Museum & Country Store
900 Wabash Avenue
Terre Haute, IN 47808
(812) 232-9446

Tour this renovated museum, country store and bake shop and learn about the history of Clabber Girl baking powder and other Hulman & Company products. Hulman family memorabilia and company relics are also on display.

TOPEKA
Yoder Popcorn
7680 W 200 S
Topeka, IN 46571
(800) 892-2170

Enjoy a free sample as you look around this cozy country shoppe that offers a variety of gifts for popcorn lovers.

WINCHESTER
SilverTowne Coin Shop
120 East Union City Pike
Winchester, IN 47394
(800) 788-7481

One of America's largest and most respected rare coin dealers, you will find an incredible coin collection of all types and dates along with quality precious metal gifts, hand-crafted original jewelry designs, and collectibles.

ZIONSVILLE
The Village of Zionsville
Chamber of Commerce
135 South Elm Street
Zionsville, IN 46077
(317) 873-3836

One of a few towns in the United States that has preserved its brick main street, the village has more than 50 shops, from uniquely fashionable to rare and vintage antiques. Nestled among the shops are numerous fine restaurants and quaint cafes.

Traders Point Creamery
9101 Moore Road
Zionsville, IN 46077
(317) 733-1700

Both kids and adults will enjoy touring this dairy farm. Watch the cows being milked, see the calves in their pen, view the pre-Civil War barns, visit the farmers market, and don't miss the upstairs cafe and dairy bar!

Indiana Golf Courses

Northern Indiana

KENDALLVILLE
Cobblestone Golf Course
2702 Cobblestone Lane
Kendallville, IN 46755
(260) 349-1550; (877) 867-4654

This Steven Burns design offers 18 scenic and challenging holes to make your golf experience a memorable one. The bent grass tees, impeccable fairways, well-manicured greens, mature trees, and sparkling water offer golfers of all abilities a fair challenge from each of four tee settings.

SOUTH BEND
Blackthorn Golf Club
6100 Nimtz Parkway
South Bend, IN 46628
(574) 232-4653

An out-of-town Notre Dame Alumni said, "It doesn't get any better than playing golf at Blackthorn on Saturday morning, then watching Notre Dame play football in the afternoon." This is a well maintained, memorable golf course near the campus.

Warren Golf Course
110 Warren Golf Course Drive
Notre Dame, IN 46556
(574) 631-4653

Nestled in a wooded grove northeast of Notre Dame's campus, the course was designed by Bill Coore and Ben Crenshaw—a heavily wooded, gorgeous tribute to the sport.

VALPARAISO
The Course at Aberdeen Golf Club
245 Tower Road
Valparaiso, IN 46385
(219) 462-5050

Created from a former horse farm, this course was rated one of the Chicago area's top courses by Chicagoland Golf for its customer service and meticulously maintained fairways and greens.

Central Indiana

CAMBY
Heartland Crossing Golf Links
South Heartland Boulevard
Camby, IN 46113
(317) 630-1785

This Nick Price designed course opened in 1998 and is known for its "high and deep sand traps." It is located five miles southwest of Indianapolis off of Interstate 465. The demanding bunkers, elevation changes, and water make this a very interesting course.

CARMEL
Prairie View Golf Club
7000 Longest Drive
Carmel, IN 46033
(317) 816-3100

Situated on the banks of the White River amid prairies lined in oaks and sycamores, this Robert Trent Jones Jr. course is a great layout. Plenty of sand, water and wetlands will allow you to use every club in your bag.

Indiana Golf Courses

CICERO
Bear Slide Golf Club
6770 East 231st Street
Cicero, IN 46034
(317) 984-3837; (800) 252-8337

Two distinctly different nines make this a uniquely different golf experience. The front nine has one tree and a true links layout, while the back side has trees, water and elevation changes. Many rate this course as one of their favorites.

INDIANAPOLIS
The Fort
6002 North Post Road
Indianapolis, IN 46216
(317) 543-9597

This surprisingly hilly course in the flat part of Indiana at Fort Harrison State Park is an exceptional golf course. The view from the tee on Hole No. 5 is one of the best in the area.

LEBANON
The Trophy Club
3875 North US 52
Lebanon, IN 46052
(765) 482-7272; (888) 730-7272

This links-style course with bentgrass fairways has plenty of bunkers, rolling greens, knee-high fescue and eight holes with water in play. Located about thirty minutes from Indianapolis, this is an excellent test of golf.

NOBLESVILLE
Purgatory Golf Club
12160 East 216th Street
Noblesville, IN 46060
(317) 776-4653

The appropriately-named course has 133 bunkers, water, and a 741-yard hole, all of which contribute to its ranking by Golf Digest as one of America's 50 toughest golf courses. Six sets of tees will allow the course to stretch from 4,400 yards to 7,700 yards.

PERU
Rock Hollow Golf Club
County Road 250 W
Peru, IN 46970
(765) 473-6100

Designed by Tim Liddy (protégé of Pete Dye) out of a former quarry, this course was named one of the best golfing values in America by Golf Magazine. Located in a rural area near Peru, this is a "must play" for the avid golfer.

SPEEDWAY
Brickyard Crossing
4400 West 16th Street
Speedway, IN 46222
(317) 492-6572

With four holes inside the Indianapolis Motor Speedway, the Brickyard is a uniquely Indiana course, and the Pete Dye design provides a challenge to match the legendary surroundings.

WEST LAFAYETTE
Brick Boilermaker Golf Complex
Kampen Course
1300 Cherry Lane
West Lafayette, IN 47907
(765) 494-3216

Be sure to play this Pete Dye gem from the correct set of tees because the links-style layout can get you with its length, not to mention heavy bunkering. Kampen also features man-made wetlands, native grasslands and large greens.

Indiana Golf Courses

Coyote Crossing Golf Club
283 East 500 North
West Lafayette, IN 47906
(765) 497-1061

The course was designed by Hale Irwin and opened for play in 2000. Many golfers feel the course is one of the best in the state and all like the new clubhouse.

Southern Indiana

BELTERRA
Belterra Golf Club
777 Belterra Drive
Belterra (Vevay), IN 47020
(812) 417-7783; (800) 594-5833

Enjoy picturesque views of the Ohio River and the hills of Southern Indiana at this parklike course designed by Tom Fazio. It features rolling hills and tree-lined fairways that meander through several man-made lakes.

COLUMBUS
Otter Creek Golf Course
11522 East County Road 50 N
Columbus, IN 47203
(812) 579-5227

This championship course is surrounded by serene countryside and designed around the gently rolling hills of Southern Indiana. Designed by Robert Trent Jones and Rees Jones, Otter Creek has hosted many of the state's top tournaments.

FRENCH LICK
Donald Ross Course at French Lick
11160 West State Road 56
French Lick, IN 47432
(812) 936-9300; (800) 457-4042

The course was originally built in 1917 and was the site of the 1924 PGA Championship won by Walter Hagen. This legendary course recently received a state-of-the-art renovation to restore its cavernous bunkers and generous greens, as well as to lengthen the tees.

JASPER
Sultan's Run Golf Club
1490 North Meridian Road
Jasper, IN 47546
(812) 482-1009; (888) 684-3287

Two hundred and twenty four rolling acres of woods, water and wildlife make this a most memorable golfing experience. The breathtaking waterfall behind #18 makes it worth the trip!

SANTA CLAUS
Christmas Lake Golf Course
County Road 1450
Santa Claus, IN 47579
(812) 544-2255; (877) 962-7465

The course has an excellent reputation among golfers the world over and is known for its beautiful tees and fairways. Rolling hills, valleys and sparkling lakes adorn the peaceful, well-manicured course.

Alphabetical Index of Restaurants

Alphabetical Index of Restaurants
(Continued)

If you would like additional copies of "DINING SECRETS" of Indiana", check with your local bookstore, gift shop, "Dining Secrets" restaurant, or call Poole Publishing.

DINING SECRETS™
of
Indiana

POOLE PUBLISHING
(317) 849-9199
(800) 401-4599

COPYRIGHT © POOLE PUBLISHING
SIXTH EDITION, 2008
ALL RIGHTS RESERVED.
ISBN: 978-0-9657499-4-7

THE CAMP-OUT MYSTERY

created by
GERTRUDE CHANDLER WARNER

Illustrated by Charles Tang

ALBERT WHITMAN & Company
Morton Grove, Illinois

ISBN 0-8075-1052-1

11

Printed in the U.S.A.

Contents

CHAPTER 1

Going Camping

"Do we have everything?" Grandfather Alden asked.

The four Alden children looked inside the station wagon. They had gotten up before dawn to pack for their camping trip. Five backpacks, one for Grandfather and one for each of the children, lay side by side. Each contained a sleeping bag, extra clothes, and a flashlight. Next to the bags were two folded tents and a cooler.

Their dog, Watch, stood on his hind legs and put his front paws on the tailgate so he could see, too. Everyone laughed.

"Don't worry, Watch," Benny, the youngest Alden, said. "I packed your food dish."

The dog's food and dishes were packed in his own special backpack. Jessie had made it for him out of an old piece of canvas.

Jessie lifted the top of the cooler. An old frying pan, stew pot, tablecloths, and dishes were packed inside.

"Is my cup in there?" Benny asked. It was right on top. No matter where he went, he always took his cracked pink cup. It was special to him. He had found it in the dump back when the children lived in the boxcar.

Violet checked her list. "What about the lantern?" she asked.

"I packed it," fourteen-year-old Henry said. "Extra batteries, too."

"Do we need a camping stove, Grandfather?" Jessie asked.

"No," Grandfather answered. "The camp provides places to make fires for cooking."

"If they didn't, we could build one," Benny said. He was six years old and a good helper.

"I guess that's everything," Violet said.

"Okay, Watch," Jessie directed her dog. "Hop in."

Watch jumped into the wagon, turned around three times, and curled up on top of a tent.

Grandfather closed the station wagon's back door. "Well, then, we're on our way."

Henry and Violet climbed into the backseat. Jessie sat in the front and opened the map. Grandfather had marked the route for her.

Benny hung back. "Wait!" he said. "Where's our lunch?" Food was Benny's favorite thing.

Jessie glanced behind her. The picnic basket was not there. "And the trail mix," she said. "We forgot the trail mix." Benny and Violet had made the blend of nuts and dried fruit the day before.

Benny started running toward the house "I'll get it," he said.

Just then, Mrs. McGregor came toward them. She carried the basket and two paper bags.

"We almost forgot the most important thing," Benny said.

Mrs. McGregor laughed. "I couldn't let you do that." She handed Benny the bags.

"This bag feels warm," Benny said.

"Your favorite cookies — just out of the oven," Mrs. McGregor explained. She handed the picnic basket through the window to Henry.

Benny climbed in beside Violet.

Grandfather started the car. "I don't know what we'd do without you, Mrs. McGregor," he said.

Mrs. McGregor stepped back. "Have a good time," she said and waved.

The children waved to her. "See you next week," they all called.

Outside Silver City, they picked up speed. Watch nudged Benny over a bit and put his nose out the window.

Benny laughed. "Watch wants to see where we're going, too," he said.

"There's another reason a dog hangs its head out a car window," Violet said. She liked animals and was always reading about them. "A dog gets nervous in a moving car. When he's nervous, he sweats. But he doesn't sweat like we do; he salivates."

Benny was just about to ask what *salivate* meant when Violet explained.

"He gets lots of saliva in his mouth and then — "

"He drools," Benny said.

Violet nodded. "But with his head out the window, he gets better air circulation," she said. "He cools off, stops sweating, and feels better."

Benny liked his explanation better. Why wouldn't Watch want to see where he was going? It was fun to see the landscape change. In just a few miles, everything looked different. The houses got further and further apart. Instead of busy towns, small quiet farms dotted the hillsides.

Violet started to hum. Before long, everyone was singing: "*A-camping we will go. A-camping we will go . . .* "

After a while, Benny stopped singing. "I'm hungry," he said. "Can we stop somewhere and have our picnic?"

The others agreed that might be a good idea. They were all getting hungry.

"There used to be a nice roadside picnic area along here somewhere," Mr. Alden said.

Jessie pointed to a sign. It said: *Picnic Area ¼ Mile.* "Is that the one?" she asked.

"It must be," Mr. Alden said as they approached the small picnic grove. He pulled off the road and parked the car. Everyone piled out. Watch ran around sniffing the ground.

The place was a mess. Empty cans and paper lay all around.

Mr. Alden shook his head. "It doesn't look like the same place," he said. "It was always so clean."

"Let's clean it up," Henry said. He began picking up cans and throwing them into the garbage can. Violet and Mr. Alden helped. Watch thought it was a game. He began bringing cans to them.

Benny found a small branch which he used like a broom to sweep off a picnic table. "That's the best I can do," he said.

"It's clean enough," Jessie said. "We have

a tablecloth." She opened the picnic basket. Inside was the blue cloth Henry had bought when they lived in the boxcar.

Jessie spread the cloth over the table and laid out paper plates and cups. She placed a wrapped sandwich on each plate: peanut butter for Benny and Grandfather Alden; tuna for Henry and Violet; cheese for herself. Violet gave each some potato chips and an apple. Henry poured milk from the thermos into paper cups.

They all sat down on the picnic benches and began eating their lunches.

"I think you'll like the campgrounds," Mr. Alden said. "I certainly enjoyed camping there when I was your age."

"Did you camp there often?" Henry asked.

"Quite often," Grandfather answered. "Camping was my parents' favorite vacation. Of course, very few people camped then. Now, it's a big thing — everyone goes camping."

"Do you suppose it'll be crowded?" Violet asked.

Mr. Alden shrugged. "Might be. This *is* spring vacation."

"Maybe we won't get in," Benny said.

"We'll get in," Mr. Alden assured him. "I made a reservation. In the old days, we didn't have to do that. We'd just pack up and off we'd go."

Back in the car, Jessie studied the map. "I think we turn up ahead," she directed.

"Sure enough," Grandfather said. "There're the old cottonwood trees."

At the corner, four large trees grew side by side. A road sign stood across from them. It read: *County B*. Mr. Alden made a smooth turn onto the unpaved road.

"Hang onto your hats," he said. "This is a bumpy one."

The children bounced as the car hit a hole in the road. They drove along the curving road for several miles. Finally, they saw a big wooden sign.

"*Blue Mound State Park*," Benny read. "We're here!"

Grandfather Alden laughed. "And now, the adventure begins!"

CHAPTER 2

Stocking Up

A grocery store stood near the entrance to the forest preserve.

"There's no store inside the park," Mr. Alden said. "We'll do our shopping here."

His tail wagging, Watch followed them to the door.

"You can't come in," Benny told him.

"Sit," Jessie said.

Watch sat.

Jessie put out her hand. "Stay," she said.

Watch cocked his head. He seemed to be saying, "I'll wait, but I don't like it."

The woman behind the counter greeted them. "Welcome," she said.

"Doris?" Grandfather asked.

The woman looked puzzled. "Yes, I'm Doris, but I don't — "

Mr. Alden put out his hand. "James Henry Alden," he said.

The woman smiled and shook his hand. "James! How nice to see you."

"It's been a long time," he replied.

"Too long," she said.

"These are my grandchildren," he said proudly. "This is Henry James. He's the oldest. He's in charge of food for the trip."

Henry smiled and held up his shopping list. "Grandfather told us we could get everything we needed here."

"Then there's Jessie," Grandfather continued. "She's twelve and in charge of the map for our camping trip."

Jessie said "Hello."

"Violet is our musician," Grandfather said. "She's only ten, but you should hear her play the violin."

Violet smiled shyly.

"It's always good to have a little music in the woods," Doris said.

"And I'm Benny," the littlest Alden said. "I'm six. I help with everything."

"I'm happy to know such good campers," Doris said.

"So, Doris, are the campgrounds crowded?" Mr. Alden asked.

"No. Things have been slow lately," Doris said. "Camping isn't what it used to be."

"How's your sister?" Mr. Alden asked. "Hildy — was that her name?"

"Yes, Hildy," Doris said. She glanced away. "She's — uh — fine."

"I remember the two of you — "

"I'd rather not talk about Hildy," Doris interrupted.

"Oh, I'm sorry," Mr. Alden said. "I hope she isn't ill."

Ignoring that, Doris came around the counter. "Let's see that shopping list," she said to Henry. "You probably want to get a move on."

They piled the groceries on the counter: bread, peanut butter, jam, milk, eggs, pancake mix, syrup, crackers, cheese, hot dogs, cooked chicken, fresh vegetables, and fruit — all the things they would need for a few days in the woods.

"The marshmallows," Benny reminded them.

"And the graham crackers and chocolate bars," Violet added.

"And the ice," Henry said.

"The ice machine is outside," Doris said.

Henry ran to get a bag. He brought it and the cooler back into the store.

They unpacked the cooler and put in the ice and the perishable items. The remaining groceries, along with the dishes and cooking things, went into two boxes.

Doris followed them to the door. "I hope nothing . . . spoils the trip for you," she said.

"I'm sure we'll have a wonderful time," Mr. Alden said as he put the boxes into the wagon.

Driving away, they waved to Doris, who was still standing in the doorway.

"What did she mean she hoped nothing would spoil our trip?" Henry asked.

"And not wanting to talk about her sister — that was strange," Jessie said.

"She was so friendly at first," Violet put in. "And then, suddenly . . ."

Mr. Alden nodded. "She did act strangely. Not at all the way I remember her."

"What was her sister like?" Violet asked.

"Hildy didn't like people very much," Mr. Alden replied. "She liked going off by herself. She lived in a cabin at the edge of the woods. The family owned it. They used it as a vacation hideaway until Hildy grew up. Then, she moved into it full time. Still, Doris and Hildy were always close." He shook his head. "It sure is a mystery," he said.

Benny sighed. "I hope not," he said.

The children laughed. They knew exactly what he meant. They liked mysteries. They were good at solving them. But they were looking forward to a peaceful camping trip with no mystery to think about.

CHAPTER 3

Checking In

Mr. Alden stopped the car just inside the park's entrance. "We have to sign in," he said.

Henry pointed to a big wooden arrow on a post. The word *Campers* was carved into it. "The arrow says campers should go to the right," Henry told him.

"I know," Mr. Alden said, "but I'm sure the ranger's station was to the left last time I was here."

"Maybe they moved it?" Benny asked.

Mr. Alden turned the car to the right. "There's only one way to find out," he said.

They drove along the unpaved road slowly. Half a mile in, the road ended.

"I guess we should have turned left," Benny said.

"Right you are," Mr. Alden agreed. He drove around the circle and headed the car back the way they had come.

When they came to the arrow, Henry said, "Stop the car, Grandfather. I'll turn the sign around."

Mr. Alden slowed to a stop.

Henry got out. He had to stretch to reach the arrow.

"Who do you suppose pointed the sign the wrong way?" Jessie asked when Henry was back in the car.

"The nail that attaches it to the post is loose," Henry said. "Maybe it just slipped around the other way."

"Could it slip that far by itself?" Violet asked.

"Violet's right," Jessie said. "If it slipped, it would point down."

"Or up," Benny put in.

"Maybe a strong wind blew it all the way around," Henry offered.

"It was probably someone playing a joke," Mr. Alden said.

Just ahead, they saw a freshly painted, green guard house. Avoiding a stack of old boards near it, Mr. Alden pulled up to the window.

The man inside the house wore a brown uniform with a state park insignia on the pocket. He smiled broadly. "Welcome to Blue Mound State Park," he said.

"We're the Aldens," Grandfather said. "I called ahead to reserve a campsite."

The man checked their name off his list. Then he handed Mr. Alden a map of the grounds. "You can have your pick of sites," he said.

Mr. Alden gave the map to Jessie. "It's your trip," he said to the children. "You choose the place."

Jessie turned in her seat so that her sister and brothers could see the map. It clearly showed the numbered campsites. Several were clustered in a clearing. Others stood alone in different parts of the woods. They quickly agreed on a location near a stand of pine with a brook running alongside. It reminded them of the place where they had found their boxcar.

Jessie pointed to the spot on the map. "May we camp here?" she asked the ranger.

"It's yours," the man answered.

"We didn't expect a choice," Mr. Alden said to the ranger. "We thought the campgrounds would be crowded. This is usually a busy time, isn't it?"

The ranger's smile faded. He looked toward the woods. "It has been, yes," he said. "In the past."

"Maybe people are getting lost," Benny said. He told the ranger about the sign.

"I'll have to check that out," the man said. He smiled again. "Well, you're all set. I hope you enjoy your stay here."

The Aldens thanked him and drove on to the parking lot beyond the guard house.

"I'm glad we're finally here," Benny said. "I'm hungry."

Jessie laughed. "It'll be a while before we eat," she said.

"Yes," Violet agreed. "We have to take everything to our campsite first."

"And set it up," Henry added.

Benny hopped out of the car. "Well, let's hurry," he said. Mr. Alden opened the back of the station wagon and Watch jumped out. His tail wagged wildly. He was obviously happy to be out of the car.

Each of the Aldens slipped on a backpack.

Jessie knelt beside Watch. She put his pack on his back and wound the straps under and over him. He stood very still. When she had buckled the straps, he turned his head to look at the pack. Then, he glanced up at her.

She laughed. "If you're going to go camping," she told him, "you have to carry your own load."

"There's still a lot to carry," Henry said. "We might have to make two trips."

Mr. Alden studied the map. "It's a long hike to our campsite," he said. "If we have to make two trips, it might be dark before we're settled."

"We'll each carry something," Benny suggested.

"The groceries are heavy," Henry said. "I don't think it'll work."

"Come with me, Henry," Jessie directed. "I have an idea."

The others waited while the two oldest ran back to the ranger's house. Shortly, they returned carrying a board.

"The ranger said we could use this," Jessie said. "It's an old board from one of the park buildings. They've been making repairs."

Henry set a box near each end of the board. The tents and their other things went in between.

"That should work," Jessie said. "The weight is even."

"Who wants to help me carry the board?" Henry asked.

"I will," Mr. Alden said.

"Violet and I will carry the cooler," Jessie suggested.

"What about me?" Benny asked. "I can carry something."

"Would you carry my violin?" Violet asked.

Benny beamed and took the case from her. "I'll be very careful with it," he said.

Violet smiled at him. "I know you will, Benny," she said.

Single file, they started off down the path to their campsite. Watch took the lead. He ran ahead, his nose to the ground. Every so often, he would stop and look back to make sure the others were coming.

The air was clear and cool. High above them, birds sang. They passed through a stand of pine. The pine needles were soft underfoot. They could hear the murmur of rushing water.

"We're nearly there," Henry announced.

And sure enough, on the other side of the pine grove was a small clearing. A perfect setting except for the cans and paper bags and plastic cups and tableware.

"Somebody must have been camping here recently," Jessie said.

"And it looks like they left in a hurry," Benny said.

CHAPTER 4

Making Camp

The Aldens put down their burdens and stared at the mess.

"Why would anyone leave a campsite like this?" Violet asked.

"Thoughtlessness," Mr. Alden answered. "People don't think about the effect they have on the environment."

Henry slid off his backpack and set it on the ground. Then, he leaned over and picked up a soda can. Following his lead, everyone chose a spot to clean up. Before long, the campsite was cleared of debris, and the garbage pail under the maple tree was nearly filled.

"Now, we can make camp," Henry said.

"The first thing to do is decide where the cooking and dining areas will be," Mr. Alden said.

Jessie walked over to a circle of large stones. Charred wood lay inside. Nearby, there was a picnic table. "How's this?" she asked.

"Perfect," Mr. Alden said.

Henry and Benny unrolled a flat piece of canvas to protect their supplies from the weather. While it was spread on the ground, they fastened the six tent poles, four to the ends and two in the middle. Next, Henry found a large stone and pounded six pegs into the ground. Then, he tied a line that extended from the top of each pole to a peg.

"Okay," he said. "Time to put up the tent."

The children raised the first two corner poles.

"Hold them steady," Henry directed as he tightened the lines.

They moved to the opposite corner and did the same. When the middle two poles were standing, the job was finished.

"Good job," Mr. Alden said, "but not quite right."

"What's wrong with it, Grandfather?" Benny asked.

"It's flat," Mr. Alden pointed out. "What will happen if it rains?"

"The water will pool on top," Henry said.

"And probably leak through," Jessie added.

"I know what to do," Henry said. He picked up his pounding rock and began driving a corner peg deeper into the ground. He did the same to three other corner pegs but not to the center two poles. When he had finished, the canvas sloped down from the middle. Now, water would run off of it.

Next, they had to choose a spot for their sleeping tent.

"How about under that tree?" Benny asked. "It'll be nice and shady."

"It would be cool there," Grandfather agreed, "but if it storms — "

"Lightning," Violet said.

"How about right here where I'm standing?" Mr. Alden asked.

The children examined the spot. It was clear — no rocks or roots or poison ivy beds — and it sloped just enough so that rain would run down and not pool.

"It's a good place for our tent," Henry said.

Watch pawed the ground. Benny squatted beside him. He saw a mound of earth with small holes in it.

"The ants thought it was a good place, too," he said. "I don't want to spoil their home."

They decided on another location nearer the brook. While Mr. Alden and the boys pitched the tent, Jessie and Violet began unpacking supplies under the canvas covering the cooking area.

"We can't just put things on the ground," Violet said.

"No," Jessie agreed. "Everything will get damp and ruined."

They gathered big rocks and made two

stacks several feet apart. These they bridged with the old park building board. It was a perfect table for the supply boxes and the first aid kit. The cooler fit underneath with room to open the lid.

The boys had done a good job, too. The sleeping tent was up and the backpacks and sleeping bags were inside.

"Now can we eat?" Benny asked.

"First we have to collect wood for a fire," Henry said.

Benny ran over to the cooking pit. "There's wood here." He pointed to a small woodpile nearby.

"I suppose that's enough for tonight," Henry said. "We'll gather more in the morning."

"You make the fire," Jessie said to Henry and Mr. Alden. "We'll find some long sticks for the hot dogs." She, Benny, and Violet ran off into the woods.

Henry made a wood teepee in the center of the pit and stuffed some newspaper inside. Mr. Alden got the matches from the tin box in the kitchen tent.

By the time the girls and Benny returned, the fire was burning nicely, and Henry had made a salad of lettuce, tomatoes, and shredded cheese, and set the picnic table.

The Aldens roasted their hot dogs.

"I'm going to put my salad on mine," Benny said. He tore some lettuce into small pieces and cut up a tomato slice. He piled them and a spoonful of cheese on his bun.

"That's a good idea," Grandfather said, doing the same.

"Save room for Mrs. McGregor's cookies," Jessie reminded everyone.

"I always have room for those!" Benny assured her.

After supper, everyone cleaned up.

"We can burn the paper plates and napkins in the fire," Henry said.

"And if we put the wet garbage at the outer edge of the fire," Jessie said, "we can burn it when it dries."

Finished with the cleanup, they sat around the fire.

"Let's tell ghost stories," Henry suggested but everyone was too tired to think of one.

Benny felt something whiz past him. He ducked. "What was *that*?" he asked.

"I think it was a bat," Henry said. He pointed upward where small dark shapes swooped.

"They're out catching insects for their supper," Mr. Alden said. "They'll be gone soon."

"It almost hit me!" Benny said.

"Oh, it wouldn't do that," Grandfather assured him. "Bats have a very good sense of direction."

"They have a kind of radar," Violet told him. "They bounce sound off objects to locate them."

"Just so *they* don't bounce off *me*!" Benny said.

They all laughed.

Bright stars filled the sky. Everyone leaned back to admire them.

Using his jacket for a pillow, Benny settled against a tree trunk. "I think I'll stay up all night and look at the stars," he decided. But he had no sooner said that than his eyes closed, and in a minute he was asleep.

CHAPTER 5

Loud Dreams

Violet awoke with a start. She thought she had heard something. She sat up in her sleeping bag. On the other side of the tent, Watch was alert, his ears up, listening. Violet seemed to be the only one of the Aldens in the big tent who was awake. She got up and peeked outside. The woods were wrapped in mist.

Jessie came up behind Violet. "What's the matter?" she asked her sister.

"I thought I heard something," Violet said. She and Jessie started toward the dining tent.

"Music?" Jessie asked.

"Loud music," Violet answered. "Did you hear it, too?"

Jessie nodded. "I thought I was dreaming. Where do you suppose it was coming from?"

Violet shook her head. "I don't know. At first, I thought it was someone's radio — another camper's maybe. But it kept getting louder. It seemed to be coming from just over there." She pointed toward the trees at the edge of their camp.

"And then it faded," Jessie said. "Maybe someone walked past *carrying* a radio."

"I don't think so," Violet said. "It was too dark to be hiking in the woods."

"Whoever it was might know the woods well," Jessie suggested. "And maybe they had a lantern."

"But why would anyone want to play loud music like that in the middle of the night? Especially if they were hiking in the woods?" Violet wondered.

"To scare animals?" Jessie suggested.

"I don't know," Violet said. "It just doesn't make sense. And I heard something else:

someone or something moving around out here. Watch heard it, too."

"Well, it's quiet now," Jessie said.

"And it's getting light," Violet added. "I don't think I can get back to sleep."

"A nice hot shower would feel good," Jessie said.

"Yes," Violet agreed.

While the others slept, Jessie and Violet got out clean clothes and followed the path to the bathhouse. It was a big building divided into two parts: one for men; one for women. Inside each section, a line of sinks faced a line of showers.

When they were dressed in clean jeans and T-shirts, they walked back to camp.

At the site, Henry was up and setting the table. "I used the plastic tablecloth," he said. "I thought we should save the blue one for dinnertime."

Henry put a bowl of fruit on the table next to the lantern. The red apples, yellow bananas, and green grapes made a colorful centerpiece.

Benny brought out the cereal boxes. "I

can't find the honey," he told the others.

"It was in the big box with the cereal and crackers," Jessie said.

Benny shrugged. "I didn't see it there."

Jessie went back to the kitchen tent with him. She glanced into the box, but she didn't see the squeeze bottle of honey either. She lifted everything out and looked inside. "That's strange," she said. "The honey isn't here."

Henry saw something on the ground next to the cooler. He reached down and picked it up. It was the honey.

"How do you suppose it got out of the box?" Jessie wondered aloud.

Benny glanced to either side of him. "Are there bears in these woods?" he asked.

·"It was probably just a raccoon or something," Violet assured him. That would explain the noise she heard.

Mr. Alden emerged from the tent. "Good morning, children," he said. "You're up early."

"Good morning, Grandfather," Jessie and Benny chorused.

"Breakfast is ready," Henry said. "I'm afraid there's no coffee, though. We didn't make a fire to heat the water."

"Orange juice and cereal are just fine," Grandfather said.

They all sat down and poured their favorite cereal into bowls. Benny sliced a banana on top of his cornflakes.

"Did everyone sleep well?" Mr. Alden asked.

"I dreamed I was listening to an orchestra," Henry said. "Suddenly, the music got louder and louder."

Benny looked surprised. "I dreamed about loud music, too," he said.

Violet and Jessie exchanged glances. "That wasn't a dream," Jessie said. "We heard loud music, too!"

"So did I," Mr. Alden put in. "It didn't last long, but it was very disturbing."

"I wonder where it came from," Henry said.

"Some camper with his radio volume turned up," Mr. Alden suggested.

"That's what we thought," Violet said,

"but it got so loud it sounded as though it were near us."

"And then it faded," Jessie added.

"Well, I just hope they don't do that every night," Benny said. "I don't like loud dreams."

Violet and Benny put the napkins and other dry garbage in the center of the fire pit, and put a log on top so it wouldn't blow away. They set the wet garbage at the edge of the pit to dry. They would burn it later.

Jessie and Henry washed off the spoons and knives in the brook.

"We'll heat water later to wash them properly," Jessie said.

"What do you children want to do today?" Mr. Alden asked.

"Go exploring!" they all said at once.

"Run along then," he said.

"Don't you want to come with us, Grandfather?" Violet asked.

Mr. Alden shook his head. "Thank you, no. I think I'd like to stay here and read." He opened a magazine he had brought with him.

"We won't be too long," Jessie said.

"Take all the time you want," Mr. Alden said. "Just don't get lost. The woods can be tricky. They can make a person lose all sense of direction."

Henry held up a silver compass. "We won't get lost with this," he assured their grandfather.

Jessie packed some fruit and trail mix for their trip. Now they were ready to go. Watch followed them to the hiking path.

"You stay here with Grandfather," Jessie told him.

"Take Watch with you," Mr. Alden said. "With him along *and* the compass, I won't worry about you getting lost."

Violet paused to look at the dark buds on the maple tree. She reached up and touched one. It felt like velvet. "These are ready to open," she said. "We've come to the forest at a very good time."

CHAPTER 6

The Missing Lantern

They hiked a long way into the woods. After a while they came to another small clearing. A camp was set up there. A woman, a man, and two small children sat at the picnic table eating breakfast. At one end of the table, a portable radio played softly.

"Maybe they played the loud music," Benny said.

"Let's find out," Henry suggested.

The man saw the Alden children. He snapped off the radio. Then, he waved.

"Hello, there," he said. "Are you camping here, too?"

The Aldens walked closer.

Henry said, "Yes, our camp is over that way." He pointed toward their campsite.

"We're the Changs," the man said. "It's nice to meet you."

Henry introduced himself and his sisters and brother.

"And this is our dog Watch," Benny added.

Watch lifted his paw.

The Chang children giggled.

Mrs. Chang said, "We thought we were the only campers here."

"It seemed a pleasant change," Mr. Chang added. "All the other campgrounds we've tried have been so crowded."

"We thought we were the only ones, too," Benny piped up, "until we heard loud music last night."

The man and woman looked at each other. "Loud music?" they both said.

"You didn't hear it?" Jessie said.

"We were awfully tired last night," Mr.

Chang said. "We slept pretty soundly. But — "

One of the children said, "More milk, Daddy," and reached for the pitcher. It tipped. Mr. Chang caught it just as it was about to fall over.

Just then, the other child slipped off the picnic bench and started to cry. Mrs. Chang rushed to pick her up.

Henry edged toward the path. "We'll see you again," he said.

The Aldens hiked along silently. They listened to the birds singing overhead. They saw chipmunks and squirrels and rabbits.

Finally Jessie said, "It sure is strange that the Changs didn't hear that music last night. Their campsite isn't *that* far from ours."

"Do you think the Changs are the ones who played it?" Violet asked.

"They have a radio," Jessie said. "They could be the ones."

"But why would they do it?" Henry asked.

"I don't know," Jessie answered.

They fell silent again, thinking.

After a while, Benny said, "I'm hungry."

"Again!" Violet said.

"You're *always* hungry," Henry joked.

"I know," Benny agreed.

Jessie pointed to a large flat rock. "Let's sit there," she said, "and eat some fruit."

"We can leave the seeds and peels here," Violet said when they had finished their snack. "The birds and small animals will eat them."

They continued on. Every so often, they found an empty soda can or some other waste. They picked it up and dumped it into their empty lunch sack.

When it was full, Henry said, "Too bad there aren't more garbage cans along the way. We'll have to carry this with us until we find one."

Before long, they came to a wide stream. Watch wagged his tail and lapped up a drink of water.

"This must be the same brook that runs along our campsite," Henry said. He took out the campgrounds map and studied it. "We're nearly out of the park," he told the others. "We'd better turn back."

They followed the stream back toward camp.

"We have to stop for wood," Henry reminded them.

There were special areas marked on the map where campers could get wood. The children stopped at one. They dropped the debris they had collected into a garbage can. Then they went to the large, tarpaulin-covered woodpile.

"How will we carry the wood back to camp?" Violet wondered.

"I have an idea," Henry said. He took off his belt. He wrapped it around several pieces of wood and buckled it. "We can carry it this way."

When the children got back to camp, Grandfather was napping against the maple tree, his magazine open beside him.

The children didn't wake him. Instead, they took off their shoes and socks and went wading in the stream. The cold clear water soothed their tired feet. They splashed it on their wrists and faces. It was refreshing.

* * *

In the late afternoon, Henry and Benny laid the fire. Then they went into the kitchen tent to prepare supper.

"Benny, you can peel and slice the carrots," Henry directed. "Jessie, you do the potatoes." He began slicing a large onion.

Grandfather came in. "What can I do?" he asked.

"You can tear up the lettuce for the salad," Violet said. "I'll set the table."

When they all had finished, Violet made hamburger patties and Henry put each one into a foil packet with some of the vegetables. Jessie lit the fire. "We don't want a big flame for this meal," Henry said. "We'll have to let it burn down a while."

While they waited for the fire to be just right, they sat at the table and had cranberry juice and crackers.

"How was your hike?" Mr. Alden asked.

"We met some other campers," Henry said.

"They didn't hear the loud music," Violet told him.

"That's strange," Mr. Alden said. "It was

loud enough to be heard all over the park."

"That's what we thought," Jessie said.

"They must be very sound sleepers," Mr. Alden said.

When most of the logs had turned to ash, Henry brought out the foil packages and Jessie set them on top of the coals. Twenty minutes after that, everyone sat down to enjoy their meal.

"This is delicious," Jessie said.

Everyone agreed.

"It's called hobo stew," Henry said.

"What are we having for dessert?" Benny asked.

"Who needs dessert after that big meal?" Grandfather teased.

"I do," Benny said.

Jessie brought out the marshmallows, graham crackers, and chocolate bars. Violet got the long, pointed sticks. Henry added wood to the fire. Benny danced around it excitedly.

"S'mores!" he exclaimed. "My favorite."

They sat around the campfire until it had burned itself out. Even then, they hated to go to bed.

"It's so quiet here," Violet said.

"And so dark," Benny added.

"I'll get the lantern," Henry said. He walked to the table. Then he called, "Where *is* the lantern?"

"The last time I saw it, it was on the table," Jessie said. It was there when Violet and I came back from our showers."

"It was there after breakfast," Violet said. "I had to move it when I took off the tablecloth."

"Then it must have been there when we left for our hike," Henry said. He made his way to the tent where he got a flashlight from his backpack. He shone it this way and that, but he couldn't find the lantern anywhere. "Someone must have taken it," he concluded.

"Why would anyone want our lantern?" Benny asked.

"How could anyone have taken it?" Mr. Alden wondered. "I was here the whole time you were gone. Do you think someone took it while I dozed?"

"Maybe," Jessie said.

"Wherever it is, we won't find it tonight," Mr. Alden said. "It's time to turn in. We'll look for it in the morning."

Suddenly Watch, who had been curled up at Jessie's feet, sat up. He growled softly.

"What is it, Watch?" Jessie asked.

"Look over there!" Benny said. "Lights!"

They all looked toward the woods. Two beams of light moved away from them. They seemed to dance through the trees. Then, just as suddenly as they had appeared, they were gone.

"What was *that*?" Benny asked.

"Maybe it's someone with our lantern," Violet answered.

"There were *two* light beams," Henry said.

"It could be people with flashlights," Jessie said. "The Changs maybe."

"What would they be doing in the woods at this time of night?' Violet asked.

Jessie couldn't think of a single reason.

Mr. Alden got to his feet. "Let's sleep on it," he said. "In daylight, things look less mysterious."

CHAPTER 7

No Pancakes for Breakfast

Next morning, Henry had the fire going by the time the others woke up. They were all surprised.

"If we had something to put the frying pan on, we could have pancakes for breakfast," Jessie said.

"We do have something," Henry told her.

Resting on two stacks of stones, a metal grill spanned the fire.

"Watch and I went looking for our lantern this morning," Henry explained. "I thought some animal might have carried it off and dropped it somewhere. Instead, we found the grill at an empty campsite."

Violet said, "Now you can have your coffee, Grandfather." Then she and Benny skipped off to fill the coffee pot with water from the pump.

Jessie went to make the pancake batter. The mix wasn't in the box. She looked all over for it. Finally, she returned to the others. "I can't find the pancake mix," she told them.

"Are you sure we bought some?" Henry asked her.

"Yes," Jessie answered. "It was in the box with the cereal."

"Maybe Benny moved it when he was looking for the honey," Mr. Alden suggested.

"I looked in both boxes. I even looked in the cooler," Jessie said. "It's not anywhere."

Returning with the coffee pot, Violet asked, "What's missing now?"

"The pancake mix," Jessie told her.

"Oh, no," Benny said. "Not the pancake mix!"

"Something strange is going on," Mr. Alden said thoughtfully.

"There's probably a simple explanation for everything that's happened," Henry said.

"A raccoon could have taken the pancake mix," Jessie said, "and knocked the honey out of the box."

"He might even have carried the lantern off somewhere," Violet added.

"That could explain the light," Benny put in. "Maybe he was running with the lantern and the light was bouncing all over the place."

"That *could* make it look like two lights when it was only one," Henry said.

"And who turned the lantern on?" Grandfather asked.

"Raccoons are very smart," Benny answered.

"Smart enough to play music?" Mr. Alden asked.

"There wasn't any music last night," Violet said.

"No," Mr. Alden said, "but I don't think we've heard the last of it."

Everyone was silent thinking about that.

Finally, Henry said, "I don't think we're in any danger."

"No, I don't think we are," Grandfather agreed, "but I'm not sure we should stay."

"Oh, please, let's not go home yet, Grandfather," Benny pleaded.

Mr. Alden looked from one to the other. "Do you all want to stay?"

"Oh, yes!" the children all said at once.

"All right," Mr. Alden said at last. "But I'm going to hike back to the store for another lantern."

"We could do that," Henry offered.

"Thank you, Henry," Mr. Alden said, "but the walk would do me good, and I'd like to talk to Doris. You stay here and enjoy the woods."

After a breakfast of scrambled eggs, Henry packed some trail mix and fruit and a thermos of coffee for Mr. Alden.

"How nice of you to pack me a lunch," Grandfather told him, "but I'll only be gone a little while."

"You'd better take it, Grandfather," Benny said. "Hiking makes a person very hungry."

Mr. Alden started toward the trail. Watch looked confused. He didn't seem to know whether to go with him or to stay with the children.

Mr. Alden laughed. "You stay here, Watch. I'll be back soon."

Watch wagged his tail. He seemed to understand.

The children decided to play hide and seek in the pine grove. Henry covered his eyes and began to count. Everyone else ran to hide. Watch followed Jessie. She found the perfect hiding place under an outcrop of sandstone.

"Shhh," she warned Watch.

The dog sat quietly beside her.

Still, Henry found them. He found Benny and Violet, too.

"So who wants to be It now?" Henry asked.

"It's too hot to play," Benny said. "Let's go wading instead."

They took off their shoes and socks and rolled up their jeans. The children laughed and splashed in the cool stream for a long time. Then they dried off in the sun.

"Let's make stew for supper," Jessie suggested. "Grandfather will be hungry after his long hike."

Jessie got the fire going.

Benny took the stew pot to the pump to fill it with water.

Henry and Violet cut up the vegetables and chunks of beef.

By the time the stew was simmering, the sky was dark with clouds.

"It looks like we're in for a storm," Henry observed.

"I hope Grandfather gets back soon," Jessie said.

Lightning flashed in the distance. After several seconds, a low rumble sounded. An hour later, the first big drops of rain fell on their camp.

But Grandfather Alden had not returned.

CHAPTER 8

The Storm

"What do you suppose happened to Grandfather?" Benny asked.

They had pulled the picnic table under the kitchen tent and were sitting at it. Rain fell all around them. In the distance, thunder rumbled. Plates of stew sat before them. No one was very hungry.

"I'm sure he's all right," Jessie said. She didn't want the others to know how worried she was.

"It's not safe to be walking in the woods during a storm," Henry reminded them.

"Grandfather probably decided to stay with Doris and her family."

"Yes," Jessie said. "That's what he did. He stayed with Doris."

"He'll be here by the time we get up in the morning," Violet added. But she was as worried as Jessie.

"Then let's go to bed now," Benny suggested, "so morning will come quicker. I don't like being here without Grandfather."

They put the leftover stew in a container in the cooler and cleared off the table.

Henry aimed his flashlight at the big tent. The others made a dash for it. When they were safely inside, he ran to join them.

Their sleeping bags felt warm and cozy, but they couldn't sleep. They lay listening to the rain drumming on the tent, each of them thinking about Grandfather. His empty sleeping bag made them feel even sadder.

After a long silence, Henry said, "Remember when we didn't want to live with Grandfather?"

"Yes, we thought he was mean," Violet said.

"And we didn't even know him!" Jessie put in.

"That wasn't very smart," Benny summed up. "He's the best grandfather in the whole world."

Suddenly, everything was light and sound. Lightning flashed. Thunder crashed. The ground shook. The children moved closer together. Benny pulled his sleeping bag up over his head.

The storm pounded around them for most of the night. When it finally moved on, Benny sighed. "I'm glad it's over," he said. He rolled over and went to sleep.

The others were just drifting off when — suddenly — music ripped through the night air.

Watch pricked up his ears. He stood up, listening. Then he moved to the tent flap and poked his nose outside.

"What is it, boy?" Henry whispered. "Who's out there?"

Watch looked at Henry over his shoulder. He yawned, turned around three times, and curled up by the door of the tent.

"The music sounds close," Jessie whispered.

"It's even louder than last time," Violet added.

Then, just as suddenly as it had started, the music stopped. The rain had stopped, too. Except for the steady *drip drip* from the trees, everything was quiet.

"Whoever's playing it doesn't want us here," Henry said.

"What makes you think that?" Jessie asked.

"Why else would they keep playing it at night like they do? And so near?" Henry said. "They're trying to spoil things for us."

" 'I hope nothing spoils the trip for you,' " Violet quoted. "Isn't that what Doris said?"

"Do you suppose she's the one who's trying to scare us off?" Jessie wondered.

"She can't be," Henry said. "She's probably with Grandfather right now."

"I hope so," Jessie said. "I hope he's warm and safe just like we are."

CHAPTER 9

Grandfather Is Missing

Jessie felt something on her arm. Half asleep, she brushed it away. She felt it again. She opened her eyes. Watch sat beside her, pawing her gently.

She sat up. "What is it, Watch? What's the matter?" she whispered.

The dog crept to the tent door where he stood with his head cocked, listening.

Jessie crawled out of her sleeping bag and tiptoed over to him. She lifted the tent flap and went outside, Watch at her side.

Henry came outside. "What's the matter?"

"Watch woke me up," Jessie answered. "I thought someone might be out here. I was hoping it was Grandfather."

"Grandfather would wait until daylight to come back," Henry said. "Watch probably heard the water dripping from the trees."

"Probably," Jessie agreed. Just as she turned to go back inside, she saw something move. "Did you see that?" she whispered.

"What?" Henry said.

She pointed to the edge of their camp. "Something moved over there in the trees."

Henry held up his flashlight. "I don't see anything," he said.

Benny came to the door of the tent rubbing his eyes. "What's going on?" he asked.

"Jessie thought she saw something," Henry told him.

Benny yawned. "It's too dark to see anything," he said and went back inside.

"He's right," Jessie said. "It was probably my imagination."

Henry and Jessie had no sooner gone back to sleep than Benny woke them. "I think we should go find Grandfather," he said.

"Let's have breakfast first," Jessie suggested. "Maybe he'll be here by the time we've finished."

They ate fruit and bread and jelly. They used paper napkins as plates so they wouldn't have to spend time washing dishes.

Afterwards, Henry looked at the map. "The path along the stream is a short cut," he said.

"If we go that way, we might miss Grandfather," Violet objected.

"But Grandfather might still be at Doris's," Jessie said. "It's early. If we take the short cut, we'll be there sooner."

Henry spread out the map. "The shortcut meets the main trail here," he said. "Even if Grandfather starts back, chances are we'll meet up with him."

"What if he comes back and we're not here?" Benny asked. "He'll look for us. We could keep missing one another all day."

"Let's leave a note," Violet suggested. She took a piece of paper and a pencil from their supplies, and wrote: *Went hiking. Back soon.* "How's that?" she asked.

Everyone agreed that was fine. They left the note in the middle of the table. Henry put a rock on it so it wouldn't blow away. Then they all started out of camp.

Benny and Watch ran on ahead. Suddenly, they stopped. The others caught up to them.

"What's the matter?" Henry asked.

Benny put a finger to his lips. He pointed across the stream. There, in the woods, something small and white flicked back and forth through the trees.

"It's a deer!" Violet whispered.

The animal bolted out of sight.

Hoping to see more deer, they kept an eye on the woods as they moved along the trail. Where the stream trail and the main trail met, they saw something else: a cabin.

"I didn't notice that cabin when we hiked to our campsite," Henry said.

Set far back in the thick clump of trees, the log house was easy to miss.

"It's hard to see," Violet said. "It blends into the woods so well."

"It needs a white tail," Benny joked.

Henry started toward it. "Maybe whoever lives there saw Grandfather. Let's ask."

Jessie hesitated. "That says '*No Trespassing.*' " She pointed to an old wooden sign.

Just then a woman came out of the cabin door. She was tall and thin and she was frowning.

"She doesn't look very friendly," Benny whispered.

Moving still closer, Henry called out, "Hello!"

The woman put her hands on her hips and glowered at the children.

"We're looking for our grandfather," Henry told her. "We thought you might have seen him pass by."

"Can you read?" the woman asked.

"Why — uh — yes," Henry said.

"Then why don't you?" she snapped. " 'No trespassing' means *no trespassing*."

"Oh, we didn't mean to break any rules," Jessie explained. "We just thought — "

The woman turned on her heel and went back inside the cabin.

"She certainly *is* unfriendly," Henry said.

"You were right about that, Benny."

"Could that be Doris's sister?" Violet wondered aloud.

The others thought about that possibility.

"Grandfather did say she lived in a cabin," Violet reminded them. "And she liked going off by herself."

The main path was full of puddles from the night's rain. Along the sides, earth had been washed down into the gullies. The children picked their way along trying to avoid the mud and deep holes.

The trail headed up the hill. Near the top, Watch pricked up his ears. He sniffed the air. For several seconds, he stood stone still. Suddenly, he broke into a run and disappeared over the crest of the hill.

"What do you suppose he heard?" Violet wondered.

"Whatever it is, he's sure excited about it," Henry said.

"He's probably chasing an animal," Benny offered.

That worried Jessie. Watch was a brave dog, but he was no match for a cornered raccoon or some other wild animal. "Watch!" she called. "Come back!"

Watch came running toward the children. He circled them, yapping excitedly. He took off again. Then he came galloping back to be sure they were following him.

In the lead, Henry picked up his pace. "Come on," he said. "Watch is trying to tell us something."

Forgetting the puddles and the mud, they all raced along the path. At the top of the hill, they looked for Watch. He seemed to have disappeared. But they could hear him barking.

"Watch! Where are you?" Jessie called.

Benny saw something move in the ravine below. He stepped to the edge of the path and looked down. "There he is!" he shouted. "And *Grandfather* is with him!"

CHAPTER 10

Rescuing Grandfather

"Grandfather!" they all said at once.

Mr. Alden was half sitting, half lying under a stone ledge at the bottom of the ravine. Watch stood beside him like a bank guard.

"Are you all right?" Violet called.

"I'm fine," Mr. Alden assured them. "Except for my ankle. I twisted it when I fell."

Henry climbed down the steep slope. The other children followed.

"Be careful," Grandfather warned them. "It's slippery."

"How long have you been here, Grandfather?" Jessie asked.

"All night," Mr. Alden replied.

"Weren't you scared?" Benny asked.

"Well, Benny, I was a little nervous." Then he said, "I don't think I can put any weight on my ankle."

"You can lean on us," Violet said.

Henry slipped Mr. Alden's arm around his neck. "That's right, Grandfather, lean on us."

Jessie and Violet took the other arm.

Mr. Alden shook his head. "Even with your help, I'd never get back up to the path."

Henry looked up toward the trail. It was a hard climb. Grandfather was right, they'd never make it. "We need help," he said.

Benny started up the slope. "Let's hurry!"

"I'll stay with Grandfather," Violet said.

"Watch, you stay, too," Jessie told the dog.

Violet took off her jacket and folded it. "Here, Grandfather, let's put this behind your head."

"You're sure you'll be all right?" Henry asked.

Grandfather nodded. "I'll be fine with Violet and Watch to take care of me."

Back on the trail, Benny said, "Let's get the ranger."

"The cabin is closer," Henry told him.

"But that woman is an old crab," Benny argued. "She won't help us."

"Henry's right, Benny," Jessie said. "Even if the woman won't help us, she might have a telephone. We can call the ranger from there."

They trekked back to the cabin and knocked on the door.

No one answered.

"Please help us," Jessie called. "Our grandfather is hurt!"

. They knocked again. Just as they were about to give up, the cabin door flew open.

"What do you want?!" the woman snapped. "Didn't I tell you to stay away from here?"

"Please let us use your phone," Henry said.

"Telephone!" the woman repeated. "You think I'd have a telephone? What would I want with a telephone?"

"Our grandfather fell down a ravine," Henry said. "We need help to get him out. Could we look around? Maybe you have something we could use to make a stretcher."

"People who can't take care of themselves should stay in the city where they belong!" she shouted. "You need help — go get Andy Watts to help you!" She waved toward the hill behind the cabin and slammed her door.

"Who's Andy Watts?" Benny wondered aloud.

Already running toward the hill, Henry said, "Let's find out."

Beyond the hill, another cabin squatted among the trees.

Henry reached it first. He knocked and called, but no one answered.

"We're wasting time," Jessie said. "Let's head back to the ranger's station."

They were just about to leave when a man carrying a long walking stick came toward them.

He smiled, "Hello, children," he said. "I'm Andy Watts. That's my cabin. What can I do for you?"

"Oh, Mr. Watts, we were looking for you," Henry said. "Our grandfather fell down a ravine and hurt his ankle. We can't get him out. Will you please help us?"

"Of course I'll help you," Mr. Watts said. He hurried into the cabin, saying, "I'll be right back." He came out with a rolled elastic bandage, which he put in his pocket. "Now, show me the way," he said.

The four of them hurried back along the trail.

"How did you know about me?" Mr. Watts asked.

"We went to the other cabin," Jessie told him. "The woman there said a man named Andy Watts would help us."

Mr. Watts nodded. "That's Hildy," he said. "She's something, isn't she?"

"Unfriendly is what she is," Benny said.

Mr. Watts laughed. "Her bark is worse than her bite," he said.

They reached Mr. Alden and Violet and climbed down beside them. Watch got between Mr. Watts and Grandfather. He growled softly.

"That's strange," Jessie observed. "He's usually friendly."

Mr. Watts said, "He's just doing his job — guarding your grandfather." Then he put his hand out toward Watch. The dog sniffed it and wagged his tail. Mr. Watts patted his head. "I like animals," he said, "so they usually like me."

Henry made the introductions, and then Mr. Watts said, "Let me see that ankle." He carefully pulled Mr. Alden's sock down. "It's swollen all right," he said. "Can you move it?"

Grandfather made a slow circle with his foot. "Yes," he said, "but it hurts."

"I don't wonder," Mr. Watts said. "It's a bad sprain. Lucky you didn't break it."

"I thought I did," Mr. Alden told him. "It got twisted under me when I fell."

"How did you fall, Grandfather?" Jessie asked.

"I waited at the store hoping the rain would stop," he said. "When it didn't, I decided to hike back anyway. I was walking along, when suddenly there was a blast of music. It startled me and I slipped. The next thing I knew, I was down here."

"The soil washes away in a heavy rain," Mr. Watts said. "They need to plant more trees along the trail."

"Why don't they do that?" Benny asked. "Then it wouldn't be so dangerous."

"Planting trees costs money," Mr. Watts answered. "People sometimes object to spending their tax money that way."

"They wouldn't if they fell down like Grandfather," Benny said.

Mr. Watts took out the elastic bandage.

"Should I take off Grandfather's shoe?" Violet asked.

"Not until we get him back to camp," the man answered. "His shoe will give him some support." He wrapped the bandage under and over Mr. Alden's shoe and up around his ankle. When he'd tied it securely, he said, "Now, let's get you out of here."

"How will we get Grandfather up the slope?" Henry asked.

"We won't," Mr. Watts answered. "There's a narrow deer path behind this stone outcrop. We'll follow that until the terrain is more even."

Henry and Mr. Watts helped Grandfather up.

"Put this arm around my shoulders," Mr. Watts directed.

"I'll take his other arm," Henry volunteered.

"The path is too narrow for three of us, Mr. Watts said. He gave Mr. Alden his walking stick. "Use this. It'll help."

"I'll carry these," Benny said as he picked up the thermos, and the lantern Grandfather had bought.

"Henry and Violet and I will go on ahead to clear the way," Jessie said.

Mr. Alden and Mr. Watts hobbled along behind them. Before too long, the trail and ravine were just about even.

"We'll go up here," Mr. Watts said.

They started up the slope, but Mr. Alden lost his balance and nearly fell.

"Henry, you and Benny go ahead of Grandfather," Jessie said. "Violet and I will be behind him."

"Good thinking," Mr. Watts said. "Henry and Benny, you take hold of the walking stick. That way you can pull us up."

"And we'll push," Violet said.

With everyone working together, they got Grandfather up the slope to the trail. But it was still a long way back to camp.

"I need to rest," Grandfather said.

"Me, too," Benny piped up.

Mr. Watts helped Mr. Alden to a tree stump. "Stay here and rest," he said. "I'll be back shortly."

When he was gone, Violet said, "Being out in the rain all night must have been awful for you, Grandfather."

"I was able to pull myself under the ledge," Mr. Alden said. "It kept me fairly dry. And I had the new lantern."

"I'll bet you got hungry," Benny put in.

"I had the lunch Jessie made for me," Grandfather reminded him. "I ate every bit of it. And the coffee kept me warm."

Watch barked. Something was moving along the trail toward them. It was Andy Watts, pushing a wheelbarrow. They were surprised to see him back so soon.

"We'll push you back to camp, Mr. Alden," Andy said. "That will make the trip easier for you." He helped Mr. Alden into the barrow.

Grandfather's legs stuck out in a funny way. The children laughed. The men laughed, too.

Henry and Mr. Watts pushed the wheelbarrow along the trail.

"Watch out for bumps!" Grandfather said.

At camp, Benny brought Grandfather's sleeping bag out into the sun. Mr. Watts eased the man onto it. Then he carefully removed his shoe and sock.

"Shall I get an ice pack?" Violet asked.

"That's a good idea," Mr. Watts said.

Violet dashed off to the kitchen tent. There she took ice from the cooler and wrapped it in a plastic bag.

Mr. Watts wrapped the ankle with the elastic bandage. "Keep it elevated," he said. "And stay off of it. It'll probably be fine in a few days."

Violet propped up Grandfather's ankle

with folded clothes and placed the ice pack on it.

"The ice feels good," Mr. Alden said. "Thank you, Violet." He looked around at the others. "Thank you, all!"

Mr. Watts said, "If you need help packing up to leave, just let me know."

"Oh, my ankle will be fine by the time we break camp," Grandfather assured him.

Andy Watts looked surprised. "You mean you aren't going home now?" he asked.

The children looked at Grandfather. They, too, thought he would want to leave. As much as they wanted to stay, they would gladly cut their trip short if Grandfather would be more comfortable at home.

"Oh, no," Mr. Alden said. "My grandchildren are having too good a time. They'll take good care of me, and I can stay off my ankle here as well as at home."

Andy looked doubtful. "Well, I have a feeling you might change you mind," he said. "If you do, you know where to find me." He walked off, pushing the wheelbarrow.

CHAPTER 11

The Note on the Tree

"There goes a good-hearted man," Grandfather said as Andy Watts disappeared into the trees.

"We were lucky to find him," Henry said.

"If it weren't for Doris's sister, we wouldn't have," Jessie said.

Grandfather chuckled. "So you met Hildy."

Benny made a face. "She's so crabby!" he said. "If I were Mr. Watts, I wouldn't live so close to her."

"Andy loves this forest," Grandfather told

them. "There aren't many private cabins in it."

"How do you know so much about him, Grandfather?" Violet asked.

"Doris told me," Mr. Alden explained. "Andy works at the sporting goods store in town. It's a long way, but he likes living close to nature."

"Did Doris tell you anything more about Hildy?" Henry asked.

Grandfather shook his head. "No, not a thing." His eyes closed.

"Grandfather?" Violet said. "Are you all right?"

"Just a little tired."

"I'll bet you're hungry, too," Benny said. "I sure am."

Mr. Alden smiled. "Why don't you children run along and make lunch?" He yawned. "I'll just rest my eyes a bit."

The children ran off to the kitchen tent.

"Mr. Watts said we might change our minds about leaving," Henry commented. "I wonder what he meant."

"Maybe he thinks Grandfather won't be

comfortable here," Violet offered. "His ankle *is* painful."

"But Grandfather wants to stay," Benny put in. "He said so."

"Mr. Watts doesn't know Grandfather," Jessie said.

"That's for sure," Henry added. "He doesn't know that once Grandfather makes up his mind, he doesn't change it easily."

"Henry, you light the fire," Jessie said. "We'll warm up the stew."

Jessie looked into the cooler. She didn't see the container with the stew. "Did you take out the stew when you got the ice?" she asked Violet.

Violet shook her head. "No," she said. "I didn't take out anything but ice."

"Where could it be?" Jessie asked.

The two girls looked all around.

At the table, Violet said. "That's funny. The note we left for Grandfather is gone."

"But you put a stone on it to keep it in place," Jessie said.

"Yes," Violet answered. "Here's the stone, but the note is gone."

Just then, Benny came running up to them. "Come quick," he said.

The girls followed him to the maple tree. Henry stood under it. He pointed. Midway up the trunk was Violet's note.

"The *hiking* and *soon* are scratched out," Jessie observed. "Now it reads: *Went home. Back never.*"

"And look what's holding the note against the tree!" Benny exclaimed.

It was a long, sharp arrow!

Henry reached up and pulled it out of the tree. "Someone is *really* anxious for us to leave," he said.

"But these are campgrounds," Jessie said. "Why would anyone want to keep campers away?"

"We aren't bothering anyone," Violet said.

"Except that nasty Hildy," Benny put in. "Everybody bothers her."

"It doesn't make sense," Jessie said. "Why would Hildy — or anyone — want us to leave?"

"That's what we have to find out," Henry said.

CHAPTER 12

Looking for Clues

They decided not to tell Grandfather about the missing stew and the arrow
in the tree.

"It'll only worry him," they all agreed.

Jessie and Benny made sandwiches instead
of stew.

After lunch, Grandfather said, "Why
don't you children run along. I'm sure you
have some more exploring to do."

They wanted to go, but they didn't like
the idea of leaving Grandfather alone.

"I'll be fine," he assured them.

Since their return to camp, Watch had stayed by Mr. Alden's side. That gave Jessie an idea. "Watch can stay with you, Grandfather," she suggested.

"There's no need for that," Mr. Alden said. "I'm sure he'd like to be with you children."

Watch pricked up his ears and cocked his head. He looked at the children and then at Mr. Alden. He seemed to be deciding what to do. Finally, he yawned and put his head back on Grandfather's chest.

Everyone laughed.

"I guess that settles that," Grandfather said.

Waving to Grandfather and Watch, the children started off.

Not far from camp, Henry said, "Let's stop here."

"Why?" Benny asked.

"We should talk about what's been happening," Henry explained. "Maybe we can figure out who's responsible."

They made themselves comfortable on a broad stone ledge.

"First we should go back over what's happened," Jessie suggested.

"We've heard music and seen strange lights," Benny piped up.

"The honey wasn't in the box where I'd put it," Jessie said.

"Food's been missing," Henry added. "And our lantern, too."

"Now, my note's been changed and pinned to the tree with an arrow," Violet concluded.

"That about sums it up," Henry said.

"Except for the loud music that startled Grandfather and caused him to fall," Violet said.

"We have to figure out who's doing these things," Jessie said.

"I think it's Hildy," Benny said.

"She *could* be the one," Henry agreed. "She doesn't like people so she might be trying to scare everyone away."

"But there are other people who could be doing it," Jessie said. "The Changs maybe."

"They do have a radio," Henry said.

"And they said they liked this campground

because it wasn't crowded," Violet reminded them. "Maybe they wanted it empty."

"But they have the children," Jessie said. "They wouldn't leave them alone to sneak around stealing food."

"How about Andy Watts?" Henry suggested.

"Not Mr. Watts!" Benny objected. "He's too kind."

"Well, you never know," Jessie argued forcefully.

"He seemed anxious for us to leave," Violet said.

"Only because of Grandfather," Henry said.

"Well, how about the ranger?" Violet suggested. "He probably knows the forest better than anyone. He could get around without being detected."

Henry shook his head. "I don't think he could be the one. If there were no campers, he might lose his job."

Jessie sighed. "It could be someone we don't even know."

"That's right," Henry said. "Maybe there

are campers we don't know about." He got to his feet. "Let's find out."

They followed the map to all the campsites. No one was at any of them. Finally, they came to the Changs' spot. Their equipment was there, but the family was not.

"They're probably out hiking," Henry said. "Let's head over toward Hildy's and Andy's. Maybe we'll find some clues."

They doubled back, stopping to check on Grandfather. He was asleep, Watch at his side.

A short distance down the stream trail, Benny saw something. He ran ahead to see what it was. Partially hidden in a clump of bushes was the wheelbarrow.

"Why would Mr. Watts leave that here?" Violet wondered aloud.

"Maybe it's not his," Henry said. "It could belong to the park staff."

"Or maybe he was too tired after helping Grandfather to wheel it all the way back to his cabin," Jessie suggested.

Benny sighed. "Well?" he asked. "Is it a clue or not?"

Everyone laughed.

When they were nearly at Hildy's cabin, Andy Watts came up the path toward them. He looked worried. "Well, hello," he said. "I hope there hasn't been another accident."

"Oh, no," Henry said. "We're just . . . exploring."

"We're looking for clues," Benny piped up.

"Clues?" Mr. Watts repeated.

Benny nodded. "All kinds of strange things have been happening."

Mr. Watts listened attentively as the children told him everything that had happened. Then, he said, "My, oh, my! How awful!"

"It's not *that* awful," Benny said. "We like mysteries."

"This is one you may not solve," Mr. Watts said. "It's been going on a while. Other campers have complained about the same things."

"Except for the Changs, we haven't seen any other campers," Jessie said.

Mr. Watts nodded. "Yes, that's what I

mean," he said. "No one stays long. They're afraid to stay."

"Oh, we're not afraid," Benny said.

Mr. Watts edged away. "I have to be going," he said. "Remember, if your grandfather decides to leave, I'll be happy to help. He should be home where he can get his proper rest."

After he had gone, Violet said. "Maybe Mr. Watts is right."

"If Grandfather wanted to go home, he'd say so," Henry reminded her.

"Let's ask Hildy if she knows what's been happening," Jessie suggested.

"She probably won't even talk to us," Benny said.

Hildy was outside her cabin, bent over something on an old table. The children called out to her. She didn't look up. They moved closer to her. She was fiddling with an old kerosene lantern.

"May we speak to you?" Henry asked politely. "Some strange things have been going on — "

"Loud music and lights and missing food," Benny put in.

"We thought you might have seen or heard something that would help us figure it out," Jessie said.

Hildy glared at them. "Imagination pure and simple," she said. "As if it isn't bad enough that my lantern is broken — "

"At least you have a lantern," Benny interrupted. "Someone took ours."

Hildy grabbed the lantern off the table. "Stop pestering me with your silliness," she snapped. She marched to her cabin door. "Go back to the city where you belong! I don't want you here!" She slammed the door behind her.

"You see?" Benny said. "She doesn't want us here."

"Mr. Watts said we should go home, too," Jessie reminded him.

"That's different," Benny argued. "He was thinking about Grandfather."

"We should be, too," Violet said. "We've been away a long time. He might need us."

Grandfather was reading when they returned to camp. "Something happened while you were away," he said.

The children looked at each other. What now? they wondered. They looked all around, but they didn't see anything different.

Grandfather laughed and pointed to the maple tree.

Violet caught her breath. "It bloomed!" she exclaimed.

Earlier, the tree was full of buds. Now, it was full of small tight clusters of green flowers. Other trees seemed to be blooming, too.

"Spring has sprung!" Benny commented.

The night was beautiful, too. The sky was clear and the stars were bright.

After supper, Violet got out her violin. She played several pieces. The one everyone liked best was "Twinkle, Twinkle, Little Star."

Finally, everyone went to bed. They were so tired that they fell asleep quickly. No one heard the loud music that sounded through the still night or saw the lights that cut through the surrounding darkness.

CHAPTER 13

More Trouble

"Yoohoo!" someone called.

"Is it morning already?" Benny asked.

Henry crawled out of his sleeping bag and looked out the tent window. "It's Doris," he told the others.

The children piled out of the tent.

"Well, good morning," Doris said. She set a box down on the picnic table.

"Good morning," the children greeted her.

Grandfather came out of the tent leaning on Andy Watts's walking stick.

"James Henry Alden," Doris said. "Just

what do you think you're doing? You should be resting."

Settled on a picnic bench, Mr. Alden laughed. "Coming to visit an old friend," he answered. "That's what I'm doing. And what are you doing? Hiking all this way when you have a store to run?"

Doris sat across from him. "Andy stopped in late yesterday. He told me about your fall. I thought you might need a few things." She turned to Henry. "There's a bag of ice in there. You'd better put it in the cooler before it melts."

Henry nodded and took out the ice.

Jessie glanced into the box. "You brought pancake mix!" she exclaimed.

"I figured you'd probably used yours up by now," Doris said.

"Somebody took our box," Benny said. "We haven't had a single pancake."

"Someone took your pancake mix?" she said, but she didn't sound too surprised.

"That's not all!" Benny told her what had been happening.

"Hmmm," was all she said.

"We asked your sister about it," Jessie said, "but she just told us to go home."

Doris nodded and glanced away. "Yes, that's what I was afraid of," she said more to herself than to the children. When she saw them all looking at her, she said, "What I mean is, other campers have complained about these very same things."

"That's what Andy Watts said," Violet piped up. "He told us we should go home."

Doris got to her feet. "Maybe it *would* be best if you left," she said. "I'll be happy to help you pack up right now."

"Oh, no, thank you, Doris," Grandfather said. "We're staying."

"Well, I was just thinking of you," Doris said firmly. "It can't be much fun putting up with all that noise and such."

"Can you stay and have breakfast with us?" Jessie asked.

"I have to get back," Doris answered. "I have some . . . business to take care of." At the edge of the camp she turned to face them. "I wish you'd change your mind about leaving, James."

Grandfather laughed. "An Alden doesn't change his mind easily," he said.

Doris frowned. "All right," she said, "but you may be sorry."

"What did she mean by *that*?" Violet asked when Doris had gone.

"Oh, that's just Doris's way," Grandfather said. "She was always very serious."

"We should put her on our list," Benny said.

"List?" Grandfather asked.

"We were trying to decide who could be doing all those strange things," Henry explained.

"We forgot about Doris," Jessie added.

"Well, you can keep her off your list," Grandfather told them.

"But she did act strangely," Henry said.

"She didn't sound at all surprised about the missing pancake mix or any of the other things," Violet said.

Mr. Alden shook his head. "It's not Doris," he said. "She would never think of such things."

The children had a wonderful time playing

in the forest and taking care of Grandfather that day. Only at night when the music sounded and the lights appeared did they think about solving the mystery. But, by then, they were too tired to try to figure things out.

The next morning, Jessie noticed they were low on bread. "That's strange," she said. "I was sure we had enough for a few more days."

"Someone must have taken it," Benny said.

Henry said, "I guess we'll just hike to the store for more."

"Not me," Benny said. "I want to stay here. Grandfather promised to read me a story."

"You and Violet go," Jessie suggested. "Benny and I will stay with Grandfather."

She made a grocery list, and Violet and Henry set off toward the store. They met the Changs in the parking lot. They were packing their van.

"Are you leaving already?" Henry asked.

"Yes, we are," Mr. Chang answered.

"And none too soon," Mrs. Chang added. "With all that loud music, we haven't had a decent night's sleep since we've been here."

Violet was surprised. "But I thought you hadn't heard the music."

"We didn't hear it the night you mentioned," Mr. Chang told them. "We were too tired to hear anything that night."

"There were those mysterious lights in the forest," Mrs. Chang said. "And our food is missing. It's been no picnic; that's for sure!"

"The last straw was finding an arrow holding a message in a tree at the edge of our camp," Mr. Chang said.

"The same things have happened to us!" Violet told them.

"Well, we've had enough," Mr. Chang said. "Be careful. Something is very wrong here."

CHAPTER 14

Hildy Disappears

At the store, Doris was pacing the floor. "You didn't see Hildy anywhere along the way, did you?" she asked Violet and Henry when they arrived.

"No, we didn't," Henry said. "Were you expecting her?"

"This is her shopping day," Doris answered. "She always comes in early so she won't run into any other customers. There's been no sign of her. I'm getting worried."

"And she doesn't have a phone," Violet commented.

"No, and I can't leave the store — it's delivery day," Doris said.

"We could stop to check on her," Henry offered.

"Oh, would you?" Doris sounded relieved.

"Sure," Violet said. "But she probably won't want to see us."

"I wouldn't ask you to do it," Doris said, "it's just that . . . well, I'm worried."

With her help, the children gathered the things on Jessie's list. Then, promising to be careful, they hurried off.

Henry and Violet raced into camp.

Breathing hard, Henry announced, "Something's happened to Hildy!"

"Whoa! Slow down," Mr. Alden said to them. "You look as though you're being chased."

Jessie and Benny took the grocery bags from their brother and sister and set them on the table.

"Sit down," Jessie said. "Catch your breath."

They sank to the picnic bench. Benny sat between them.

Grandfather hobbled over and sat down, too. He gave the children time to calm down before saying, "Now, tell us what happened."

Violet started at the beginning. "We met the Changs in the parking lot," she said. "They were leaving because they couldn't stand the music and the other things that have been happening."

Henry picked up the story. "And then we went to the store. Doris was upset because Hildy hadn't come in for her groceries."

"Maybe she'll be in later," Grandfather said.

Violet shook her head. "Doris said today is her shopping day, and she *always* comes in first thing."

"We said we'd check her cabin," Henry told them. "But we wanted to bring the groceries back first."

"And get you two and Watch," Violet said to Jessie and Benny.

"That was smart," Grandfather said.

"There's safety in numbers. I only wish I could go with you."

"Oh, don't worry, Grandfather," Henry said. "We'll be all right."

Benny shot to his feet. "Well, what are we waiting for?"

The four children hurried along the stream path. Watch yapped at their heels.

Hildy's cabin looked deserted. The children approached it slowly. At the door, Henry knocked.

No response.

He knocked again. "Hildy!" he called. "It's the Aldens. We have a message from Doris."

Still no answer.

"Try the door," Jessie suggested.

Henry turned the knob. The door was unlocked.

Slowly, cautiously, Henry pushed the door. It creaked as it swung open.

A few bars of light from the window fell across the cabin floor. Otherwise, the cabin was dark.

"Hildy?" Henry called softly.

He stepped inside the cabin. The others

followed. Watch ran around sniffing.

Pointing to a small table under the window, Benny said, "Look! Our missing lantern!"

A battery-powered lantern stood in the center of the table.

Henry took a few steps forward. "It looks like our lantern all right," he said.

"There are lots of lanterns like that," Violet said.

"But Hildy had a kerosene lantern," Benny reminded them.

"And it was broken," Jessie remembered. She went to the table and picked up the lantern. She turned it over. "It's our lantern, all right," she said. She showed the others the name *Alden* scratched on the bottom.

"Hildy took it!" Benny concluded. "She *is* the one behind everything!"

Henry wasn't convinced. "But our lantern was missing *before* we saw Hildy with her broken one."

"Maybe she already had our lantern here in her cabin," Violet suggested.

"But if she had our lantern, why would

she be so upset about hers being broken?"
Jessie asked.

"We don't have time to think about it
now," Henry said. "We promised Doris we'd
find Hildy."

They went back outside. Benny and
Watch ran around the outside of the cabin
looking for some sign of Hildy, but they
found nothing.

"Maybe she's on her way to the store right
now," Violet suggested. "Or already there."

"In that case, we're wasting our time," Jessie said. "Let's go back to camp."

"Not yet," Henry said. "I think we should
look around a little more."

"Let's go to Andy's," Benny suggested.
"He might know where Hildy is."

They ran over the hill, Watch in the lead.

Andy's place was closed up tight. Even the
windows were shuttered.

When the children knocked, there was no
answer.

"They're both missing!" Benny said.

CHAPTER 15

The Prisoner

Henry stepped back from Andy's cabin. "The way it's all boarded up, it looks like he's left for good," he observed.

They trooped around the side of the cabin. In back, they saw the wheelbarrow leaning against the wall.

"What's that over there?" Benny asked.

"It's a bale of hay with something on it," Violet observed.

A square white card was pinned to the bale. Painted on it were several circles, one inside the next.

"It's a target," Henry said. "The kind archers use to practice."

"Bow and *arrow* practice?" Benny asked.

Jessie knew what he was thinking. "Just because Mr. Watts likes archery doesn't mean he's the one who put that arrow in the maple tree," she said.

"That's right," Henry agreed. "Someone could have taken the arrows from him."

"Maybe Andy and Hildy are in this together," Benny said. "Maybe that's why they're both missing."

Watch pricked up his ears. He stood listening, and then he loped off toward the cabin.

The children followed him.

"He heard something," Jessie said.

Whining softly, Watch scratched at the door.

Henry knocked loudly. "Mr. Watts!" he called. "Are you in there?"

When no one answered, Benny put his ear to the door.

"There's someone in there," he whispered. "I can hear something."

The door opened a crack. Andy Watts peeked out.

"Oh, children," he said. "I'm sorry I didn't hear you." He yawned. "I was napping."

"We're looking for Hildy," Henry told him. "Have you seen her?"

"No, no, can't say that I have," he answered.

A muffled thump sounded from inside.

Mr. Watts cleared his throat loudly and began coughing.

"I — uh — can't talk to you right now," Andy said. "You run along and I'll see you later."

He closed the door but not before they heard someone yell, "Help! Help! Help me!"

"That's Hildy's voice," Jessie said.

Henry knocked furiously. "Mr. Watts! What's the matter?! What's going on in there?!"

Henry started away from the cabin. "Come on!" he said. "We'll get the ranger!"

Just then they heard a car approaching.

"It's coming from over there!" Benny ran toward a thick stand of trees. He dashed through them, the others close at his heels.

Beyond was a dirt road. The children waved frantically at the oncoming truck. It pulled up beside them and stopped.

Doris hopped out. "What's the matter?" she asked.

"Hildy," the children said at once. "She's locked in Andy's cabin!"

Doris leaped out of the truck.

They all ran back the way they'd come.

Doris pounded on the cabin door. "Andy Watts, come out here this instant!" she demanded. "Or we're going to break this door down!"

The door flew open. "All right! All right!" Andy said. He came outside, trembling.

Doris dashed into the cabin.

The children waited at the door.

Andy Watts paced back and forth. "Oh my, oh my," he kept mumbling to himself.

Finally, Doris came out with Hildy at her side. Hildy looked furious.

"Now, Andy Watts, let's hear your explanation for all of this!" Doris demanded.

CHAPTER 16

The Confession

Andy took a deep breath. "I didn't mean any harm," he said. "I just wanted to give them a taste of their own medicine."

"Who are you talking about?" Doris snapped impatiently.

"Those awful campers," Andy said. "The litter everywhere. They don't care about the forest. They just come here to make noise and mess things up."

"He stole a lantern from the Aldens," Hildy piped up.

"But our lantern is at *your* cabin," Henry said.

"Mine's broken," Hildy explained. "There's no electricity in my cabin. Without a lantern it gets awfully dark. Andy gave me one to use. When I saw your name on it, I began to wonder how he got it."

"So you came over here to question him?" Doris asked.

"I did," Hildy answered. "But when I started asking questions, Andy pushed me into the bathroom and locked the door. I *knew* then that he was the guilty party."

"When did you take the lantern?" Henry asked. "It was there in the morning and, later, it was missing. But Grandfather was at the camp the whole time."

Andy Watts shrugged. "I just waited until he fell asleep. Then I sneaked over and . . . took it. I figured without a lantern, you'd go home."

"You played the loud music, too?" Violet asked.

"Yes, yes," Andy said. "For years, I've had to listen to it. Loud music, loud voices —

any time of the night. The forest is a quiet place. People should respect that. I just wanted to let people know how it sounded. But I never meant to cause Mr. Alden's accident. That made me feel real bad!"

"And the lights?" Jessie asked. "Why did you do that?"

"To scare people away," Andy explained. "That's why I took the food. People get edgy when strange things like that happen. It worked, too. Word got around. Campers have been staying away."

"But how could you take our food when we were right there?" Jessie asked.

"You were difficult," Andy admitted. "I dropped the honey when I heard someone rustling around in the tent."

"That was me," Violet said. "I thought I heard something. I came out to look."

"I just got away in time," Andy said. "And the morning when I took the stew — "

"I saw you!" Jessie interrupted. She turned to Henry. "Remember, Henry? Watch woke me up and then I saw something moving in the mist."

"I was sure you'd catch me that time," Andy said.

"And the arrows? Did you do that, too?" Benny asked.

"That's the first thing I did: turn the wooden arrow that pointed to the ranger's station in a different direction. A few people got so confused, they left. But most people figured it out," Andy said.

"I mean the arrow in the maple tree," Benny persisted.

"Yes," Andy admitted. "I did that, too. When I returned from your campsite, you children were at my cabin."

"That was the morning we found Grandfather in the ravine," Henry said putting the pieces together.

"I only meant to scare you . . . nothing more," Andy said.

"You know, you weren't the first to complain about strange things happening," Hildy said to the Aldens. "I never believed it. Thought it was nonsense. Imagine my surprise when I realized the lantern was yours. And then to find out that Andy Watts of all people was causing so much trouble!"

"She wanted to tell the authorities what I'd done," Andy said. "I couldn't let her do that, could I? They'd put me in jail!"

"And that's why you locked her in your bathroom," Doris concluded.

"I would've let her out," Andy said. "I decided to pack up — get out of here. Go someplace where no one could find me. I would've let her out when I was ready to go." He looked from one to the other. His eyes were sad. "I didn't mean any harm," he said. "Please, believe me."

"Mean it or not, Andy Watts, you did cause harm," Doris said. "You ruined people's camping trips and the park's reputation. Something has to be done about it."

"Oh, I know," Andy said. "It was foolish of me to think of running away. I knew that even while I was packing to go. This is my home. I'd never be happy anywhere else — especially after what I've done." He sighed deeply. "I'll go turn myself in to the ranger."

CHAPTER 17

A Problem Solved

The next night, Doris and Hildy joined the Aldens around the campfire.

"It's hard to believe that Andy Watts caused so much trouble," Doris said.

"I think I understand what he did," Hildy said. "I've felt the same way about some campers. So many of them just don't appreciate the beauty around them."

The children stared at her. She seemed an entirely different person than she was before.

She smiled at them. "Are you having trou-

ble believing old Hildy likes nature?"

"We didn't think you liked anything!" Benny said.

"Now, Benny, mind your manners," Grandfather warned, but he said it lightly, and Benny knew he was amused.

"Hush, James Henry," Hildy said. "I deserved that. I wasn't very nice to your grandchildren — or to anybody for that matter. But I've learned my lesson. These children taught me. Independence is important, but so is knowing people care."

"You know, Hildy," Doris said, "for a while I was afraid you were the one causing all the trouble."

Hildy chuckled. "My own sister!" she teased. "You should have known better. My way of dealing with the campers was to ignore them. Keep my distance."

"Well, things will be different now," Grandfather said.

"They sure will be," Doris said. "Andy did a good thing by turning himself in. Things went easier for him because of it."

"I hope they aren't going to put him in

jail," Benny said. "He might have done bad things, but he's a good man."

"That's exactly what the ranger said," Doris told him. "He came up with a plan to have Andy educate and help campers. It'll accomplish a lot more than a jail sentence would."

"What exactly will he teach the campers?" Violet asked.

"He knows all about the forest," Doris answered. "He'll take people on nature hikes, and teach new campers about safety procedures and anything else they might want to know."

"I hope he teaches them about neatness," Benny piped up. "This place was a mess when we got here."

"I wish we could help," Jessie said.

"You already have," Doris reminded her. "You solved the mystery. Now, campers won't be afraid to come here."

"But we'd like to do more," Violet said.

"Maybe we can," Grandfather said. "Andy mentioned the need for more trees to keep the soil from eroding. I'll donate some."

"We could come weekends and help plant them," Henry suggested.

"That's a fine idea, Henry," Grandfather said. "I'm sure the ranger would approve."

"And the park needs more garbage cans," Jessie said. "That would help people to be neater."

Mr. Alden nodded. "We'll get those, too."

"Maybe we could set up a recycling center with different bins for bottles and cans," Henry said.

"I'll talk to the county officials," Doris offered. "They have special trucks to collect recyclable material."

"I have another idea," Benny said. "Something we can do right now to help some campers."

They all looked at him.

"Roast marshmallows and have some more s'mores," he said.

They all laughed.

"Now, that's what I call an excellent idea!" Grandfather said.

And everyone agreed.

GERTRUDE CHANDLER WARNER discovered when she was teaching that many readers who like an exciting story could find no books that were both easy and fun to read. She decided to try to meet this need, and her first book, *The Boxcar Children*, quickly proved she had succeeded.

Miss Warner drew on her own experiences to write each mystery. As a child she spent hours watching trains go by on the tracks opposite her family home. She often dreamed about what it would be like to set up housekeeping in a caboose or freight car — the situation the Alden children find themselves in.

When Miss Warner received requests for more adventures involving Henry, Jessie, Violet, and Benny Alden, she began additional stories. In each, she chose a special setting and introduced unusual or eccentric characters who liked the unpredictable.

While the mystery element is central to each of Miss Warner's books, she never thought of them as strictly juvenile mysteries. She liked to stress the Aldens' independence and resourcefulness and their solid New England devotion to using up and making do. The Aldens go about most of their adventures with as little adult supervision as possible — something else that delights young readers.

Miss Warner lived in Putnam, Connecticut, until her death in 1979. During her lifetime, she received hundreds of letters from girls and boys telling her how much they liked her books.